12                                          400

# DEMYSTIFYING
# THE MYSTICAL

# DEMYSTIFYING THE MYSTICAL

Understanding the
Language and Concepts
of Chasidism and Jewish Mysticism

A Primer for the Layman

Chaim Dalfin

JASON ARONSON INC.
*Northvale, New Jersey*
*London*

The author gratefully acknowledges permission to use the glossary from *Anticipating the Redemption,* trans. Rabbi Eliyahu Touger and Rabbi Sholem Ber Wineberg, copyright©1994 Sichos In English. Used by permission of the publisher.

This book was set in 12 pt. Garamond by AeroType, Inc., Amherst, New Hampshire.

**Library of Congress Cataloging-in-Publication Data**

Dalfin, Chaim.
    Demystifying the mystical : understanding the language
and concepts of Chasidism and Jewish mysticism : a primer for the
layman / Chaim Dalfin.
        p.   cm.
    Includes bibliographical references and index.
    ISBN 1-56821-453-7
    1. Mysticism—Judaism.  2. Hasidism.  I. Title.
BM723.D25   1995
296.7'12—dc20

                                                                 95-16069

Manufactured in the United States of America. Jason Aronson Inc. offers books and cassettes. For information and catalog write to Jason Aronson Inc., 230 Livingston Street, Northvale, New Jersey 07647.

Dedicated to the eternal life and spirit of my beloved
and revered Teacher, Master, and Father, the sainted
**Lubavitcher Rebbe**
**Rebbe Menachem Mendel**
ben HaRav HaGaon, HaChasid, v'HaMikubol,
Reb Levi Yitzchok
**Schneerson**

11 *Nisan* 5662 – 3 *Tammuz* 5754
April 18, 1902 – June 12, 1994

# Contents

# Acknowledgments

After writing my first book, *Your Better Self,* I realized there was a great need in the Jewish community to understand the basic language and terms mentioned in Chasidus and Kabbalah. I began teaching a class on this exact topic to people who were professionals. The feedback I got was very encouraging. People with very little background in Chasidus were finding amazing answers to issues and questions that had been on their minds for quite a while. It is these people who made me decide to pursue writing my manuscript. To you my students, I say thank you. As the Mishnah says, "Much I learnt from my teachers, but even more did I learn from my students."

The individual who most inspired and showed me how to implement the ideas of Chasidus in my daily activities was the Lubavitcher Rebbe, Rabbi Menachem Mendel Schneerson, of blessed memory. The years, months, days, and hours the Rebbe shared with my peers and myself through his *farbrengens,* private audiences, and writings, gave me the ability to go forward and write this book. It is the Rebbe who truly taught me to have the determination to finalize this project in a manner that necessitated alacrity.

I also thank my *mashpia,* that is, my spiritual counselor, Rabbi Yoel Kahan. "Reb Yoel" taught me how to bring alive, in the real, practical world, the words written in books. He allowed me to spend time with him as he shared with me the proper way of understanding the concepts of Chasidus. As he is extremely knowledgeable in the field of chasidic philosophy, I can say with confidence that he showed me how to understand the Rebbe's words.

I give thanks to my parents, Reb Aron Hillel and Miriam Dalfin, who raised me in such a manner that being a Jew, a *chasid,* was of greatest importance. They helped me along in my teen years, allowing me to immerse myself in the "ocean" of godliness. My mother, may she live and be well, encouraged me to write when I was eight years old. My father taught me, through sharing his experiences as a child in the Holocaust and later as a poor immigrant student in Israel, an intense love for Chasidus. In addition to my parents, my grandparents, of blessed memory, Hinda Fraida and Shlomo Menashe Wiroslaw, were influential in my development as a child. Their loving-kindness and warmth has permeated my entire being.

The *Zohar* says that a man's wife is his other half, and without her he is incomplete. Therefore my wife isn't just family; she is part of myself. My wife, Bashi, may she be well, was my guiding light as I wrote this book. Her constant thoughtfulness and constructive criticism made this book worthwhile material. She made it possible for me to spend many hours at my computer, away from the home, while she spent time educating our precious four children. To her I say a very special thank you. My four precious children, Menachem Mendel, Shterna Sara, Brocha, and Hinda Fraida, gave me the constant excitement and energy to stimulate my thinking and emotional well-being. To them I say, *Chazak vemotz,* All the power to you, *Ad meah vesrim,* Until one hundred twenty and beyond!

Thanks also go to a number of other friends and acquaintances: to Avrohom Modes, who helped edit the manuscript; to Mr. Arthur Kurzweil, vice president of Jason Aronson Inc., who recognized the valuable information contained in the manuscript and its potential and authorized its publication; to Carmen Tellev, who transcribed parts of the manuscript; and finally, to my dear brother Anshel and his business partner Yossi, who sponsored my writing and work within the Jewish community and made it possible for me to write this book with a peaceful mind.

Last but not least (as the Talmud says, "the last one is the most beloved"), I say a big thanks to God Almighty, who gave me the strength and health to write this manuscript. I pray with God's help that this book will inspire people to get in touch with their true essence as it is illuminated by the teachings of Chasidus. May we all witness the coming of our righteous *Moshiach,* when all of Israel will be reunited in Jerusalem, culminating with *Tichiyas HaMeisim,* the resurrection of the dead, when all souls that have departed will once again be here in a body. Amen.

# Introduction

Why another book on Jewish mysticism–Chasidus?
There are so many fine and valuable books explaining
this wonderful tradition, why spend your time reading
this book? The reason came to me one *Shabbos* morning after having immersed myself in the *mikvah,* a
ritual bath, as a preparation for the morning service. As
I was leaving the *mikvah* I noticed a *chasid* dressed in
the distinctive garb of his group. I asked him if he had
studied some Chasidus as a preparation for prayer, as is
the tradition by *chasidim*. He said yes. So we began
talking about Chasidus. In the midst of our conversa-
tion I asked him if he knew what the ten *sefiros* are. He
said no; all he knew was that there were ten but what
they are and what is their meaning, he had no idea. So I
took the big plunge and asked him in a respectful manner, "You're a *chasid,* you go to the *mikvah,* you say
you study Chasidus, yet you don't know the very basics
of Chasidus on the tip of your tongue?" His response

was, "That is the way we were taught, to know the words of Chasidus; however, to really understand, that's not for everyone."

As I grew older I realized that this wasn't the only issue. Many very fine and knowledgeable people study Chasidus and know the terms, yet they don't understand the lofty concepts in a real down-to-earth way. It is noted in *Tikkunei Zohar* (VI: 23b–24a), "And many people . . . shall be sustained (*yitparnessun*) by this work of [Rabbi Shimon Bar Yochai] when it will be revealed in the last generation, at the end of days, and in the merit thereof, 'You shall proclaim liberty throughout the land' (Leviticus 25:10)." The word *yitparnessun* comes from the Hebrew word *parnassah*, meaning sustenance. The way in which self and others are sustained is through internalizing the sustaining task to the point of mastering it. The result is success, and therefore reward, the reward being the money or objects needed to sustain self or family. Similarly, Chasidus needs to be studied in a manner that is internalized. This is only possible by understanding the depth of Chasidus through analogies, parables, and examples. In this way Chasidus becomes food for thought. It can be digested. It supplies the appropriate words to show how these very same esoteric thoughts are really very practical and down-to-earth. For this reason I've called the book *Demystifying the Mystical*.

This applied study is actually in accordance with the basic thrust of Chasidus from the beginning. Both the Baal Shem Tov, the founder and inspiration of the whole chasidic movement, and the Alter Rebbe, the founder of Chabad Chasidus, began with highly abstract thoughts and brought them down to the real world. This is unique in Jewish thought because Jewish mysticism, usually known as Kabbalah, is almost entirely *mufshet*, abstract. The esoteric tradition deals with concepts of worlds, processes, and levels of being that are never visible or tangible. On the other hand, classical Jewish thought, exemplified in the Talmud and the Jewish legal tradition, is almost entirely *muchshis*, tangible, dealing with things that are visible and real—a lost object, a marriage, a holiday celebration. Chasidus is neither Kabbalah nor Gemara (nor is it, strictly speaking, philosophy, which is known as *chakirah*). Chasidus, as the Rebbe says in *On the Essence of Chassidus*, is like a fifth dimension to Torah that really is the essence and core of every other part of Torah.

Therefore, my goal in writing this book is to create a primer for the average layman who doesn't have the words and explanations to make Chasidus as understandable as Talmud or the Code of Jewish Law. One doesn't have to be a *chasid* to read this book. The only prerequisite is to be open enough to pursuing the words of the *Zohar*, "And because in the future Israel will taste from the Tree of Life, the *Sefer HaZohar*, they will leave exile with it, in mercy." Chasidus, being the application of the Tree of Life, will bring the ultimate revelation of the righteous *Moshiach*, and since each and every Jew naturally desires the manifestation of *Moshiach*, therefore the study of Chasidus must be pursued, similar to the pursuit of work, health, and family.

In this vein, I feel that my book is a very much needed addition to the already existing market on the topic of Chasidus. You, my dear readers, are the only ones to assist me in this task. Read the book and tell me if the concepts flow, if you understand them easily. To make the book more simple, I've put the basic terms used in each chapter at the beginning, following the

chapter title. I have also included a list of questions for
each chapter in the appendix at the end of the book.
The questions will help you review and see for yourself
if you really understand the material. I've also included
a list of suggested books for you to read as a means to
further your understanding of the terms discussed in
my book. The Talmud says in regard to the words of
Torah, "They are poor [briefly explained] in one place,
yet they are rich [elaborately explained] in another
section of the Talmud." I say the same in regard to my
writing: there are certain ideas in the book that I have
not elaborated upon, relying on the preexisting written
works currently available on the market. I do hope to
make this work the first of a series, to further examine
other terms scattered throughout Chasidus and Kabbalah. All I ask is that God provide the strength and good
health for my family, myself, and all of Israel, culminating with the coming of our righteous *Moshiach,* now!
This will enable all of us to have the peace of mind to
continue dispersing the wellsprings of Chasidus and to
continue studying Chasidus in a manner called *yitparnessun.* Amen!

# I
# MIND AND HEART

# 1

# *Halbashah* and *Hafshotah:* Embodiment and Abstraction

## Terms

*Metzius*     Entity
*Mugdar*     Defined
*Mah shehu*     What is it
*Mah she'eino zuloso*     What it is not
*Yedias hachiuv*     Positive knowledge
*Yedias hashlilah*     Negative understanding
*Etzem hanefesh*     Absolute essence of the soul

What follows is a discussion of two basic concepts. One concept is *halbashah,* literally meaning "enclothement," but more understandable in English as "embodiment." The word is related to *l'halbish,* to put on a garment, from the Hebrew word *livush,* garment. Second is *hafshotah,* or abstraction, to strip and remove the garment.

Understanding of these terms begins with the process by which things are defined and distinguished. A first example might be what seems a simple statement.

3

It is taught in Chasidus that every *metzius* is *mugdar*. *Metzius,* loosely translated, means an existence, or better, an entity. *Mugdar* means defined, from the word *geder,* meaning fence. Just as a fence sets the boundaries of a property and it also limits and defines the property, so too every entity is limited to its description and definition.

This has both a positive and a negative aspect. When I say this is a table, I am saying two things: this is a table and it is not a chair. Those would be the limitations and definitions of my statements. This is a table and it is not something else.

The terminology for that in Chasidus is that every *metzius* is *mugdar,* described with its limitation in two aspects. The two aspects are called *b'mah shehu,* with what it is, and *mah she'einu zulosoh,* what it is not—in particular, how it is different from the other item that you are comparing it to.

Imagine that there are two people, Reuven and Shimon, who are identical in their character, behavior, and intelligence. There is a third person, Levi, who is Reuven's friend and who likes Reuven very much. But he does not particularly like Shimon. For some reason, he tends to like and relate to Reuven more than Shimon.

How do you think Reuven comes to this determination? This is an example given by the previous Lubavitcher Rebbe, who explained that the reason Levi drifts more to Reuven than to Shimon even though they outwardly seem exactly alike is that deep down in the core and essence of Levi's soul, there is an affinity to Reuven and not to Shimon. The only aspect of this that is perceived and recognized by the mind is that Reuven is not Shimon. Does Levi really understand with his mind and heart what Shimon is, how Shimon is different from Reuven? The answer is no. The one thing Levi does know is that Shimon is not Reuven because they are two separate people. So he can describe their difference negatively—Shimon is not Reuven—but he cannot describe in any positive way how Shimon is different from Reuven.

This in Chasidus would be called *yedias hashlilah*. *Yedias* means the knowledge of *shlilah,* the negative. Levi does *not* have *yedias hachiuv,* a positive understanding of how Shimon is different from Reuven. All he can say that he feels it and that for some reason he moves toward Reuven rather than Shimon.

Chasidus explains that this comes from the *etzem hanefesh,* meaning the absolute essence of the soul. The *etzem hanefesh* feeling that Levi has for Reuven versus Shimon is expressed only through *yedias hashlilah,* knowing the negative. The positive is simply, "I know who you are." Levi cannot articulate the difference, however; he knows only one thing, that they are two separate people. So as far as the intellect and the heart are concerned, he does not understand the difference. They act alike, they are alike, they understand alike, they feel, and so on.

So what does he have? He has *yedias hashlilah*. He knows what something is not; he doesn't know how they are different but he does know that there is a difference by the mere fact that they are two separate people. This causes him to make the distinction between the two people.

To put it another way, when a person ascertains that whatever the particular idea may be and mean, this he doesn't know; however, he does know what it *doesn't* mean. This we can call the divesting process, and it is also known as *yedias hashlilah*.

But how is it possible that a person could come
to know what he does not seem to be able to know?
How can the ordinary mind ever grasp the higher idea
that the soul seems to be expressing? And how can
anyone understand the person's deep emotional involvement in something that cannot be understood?
This is a very important process, relating very elevated
perceptions to the ordinary world. It is essential, for the
sake of growth and change, that the higher aspects of
soul or mind be related to the person's ordinary
existence.

The previous Rebbe describes two different approaches to this problem of relating different levels to
one another. These are the concepts of *halbashah* and
*hafshotah,* the abstraction approach and the embodiment approach.

The different approaches can be illustrated with
the following example: Efraim is on top of a mountain
and Michoel is at the base. Efraim wants to give something to Michoel. How will he do this? Either Efraim
can go down to Michoel or Michoel can go up to
Efraim; or they can meet in the middle.

This example can be applied to the process of
understanding ideas and thoughts. First, consider the
embodiment approach. Assume that the subject to be
understood is very elevated—a Torah concept, for example, or, in secular studies, a mathematical theorem.
"Elevated" here means at some distance from practical
life or observable facts. In such an instance, the idea is
the higher and the thinker is the lower. When the
higher, the idea, descends to the plane of the lower, this
is what is called "embodiment." The idea is explained
through illustrations and parallels so that it can be
grasped by the thinker. In the relationship between

mind and thinker, the idea, which exists in the mind, is higher than the thinker. When we talk about the descent of the higher to the plane of the lower, we mean that the descent includes the embodiment of the idea in illustrations and parallels. Chasidus has many, many illustrations called *mosholim,* or analogies, examples and parables. These are more concrete expressions to help us understand what the theoretical idea is all about.

The second approach is that the thinker, who is the inferior, elevates himself to the higher. Michoel, at the bottom of the mountain, walks up to the higher—to the idea. This is called an elevation. This elevation is a very sophisticated process that necessitates the refinement of the mind, making it capable of receiving delicate ideas. This comes through practice in abstracting the core of an idea from its various expressions. This is called the process of abstraction, or *hafshotah*.

For this process of abstraction, one must have a powerful mind and a familiarity with the processes of thought. It is a precarious path fraught with the possibility of error. When a person starts delving into thought deeper and deeper, the person not accustomed to delicate thinking will get confused.

Imagine Einstein developing his theory of relativity: he approached it by elevating his mind, developing his ability to comprehend more and more difficult concepts and formulas until he leaped into a totally new way of thinking. Normally, the human mind is limited to what it understands, how to get from A to B. Einstein had to develop his mind until he refined his mind, in a sense, so that he was able to come up with these very unusual thoughts. This can be true of any individual. But, as the previous Rebbe says, it does necessitate a familiarity with the process of thought, for example, with logic, correct reasoning, how to explain one thing from another, and so forth. One actually has to know how thinking proceeds. Otherwise, a person can easily become confused.

# 2

# *Sechel* and *Middos:*
# Intellect and Emotions

**Terms**

| | |
|---|---|
| *Sechel SheBeMiddot* | Intellect within emotions |
| *Middos SheBeSechel* | Emotions within intellect |
| *Middos Al Pi Sechel* | Emotions guided by intellect |

Explaining the third and ultimate method requires clarification of the overall concepts of *sechel, middos shebesechel,* and *middos.* To cite an example from Chasidus: King David says in *Tehillim,* "*Kirvat Elokim li tov:* the nearness of God is good to me." There are three aspects operative here: (1) God, Elokim, as an abstract thought; (2) *kirvat Elokim,* the closeness of God, which means within the intelligence of the individual, the individual feels a closeness but it is still removed from his or her practical life; and (3) *li tov,* it is good to me, it is something I can feel a desire for.

To put it in other terms: when you experience something, you can react in three ways. You can respond with "You know, all I see here is godliness, all I see here is intelligence." This is called total abstraction, complete *hafshotah,* removed from the real world of emotions. The second reaction is an intermediary step where you say, "Hashem is not only an intellectual concept that excludes feelings and emotions; rather I can recognize such a thing as closeness to God." This is called *middos sheb'sechel,* the emotions within the mind. The mind recognizes, beyond the intellectual, such a thing as closeness, fear, anger, or love. It doesn't say "*I* fear" or "*I* love." It doesn't say "*I* want to be close," because there isn't an actual emotion felt in the heart. All there exists at this level is the notion and idea of love or fear because, since the intellect is operative, it absorbs the notion, not allowing it to express itself in the heart. This is what is meant by having an overpowering intellectual experience. The third reaction is, "The closeness of God is good *for me,*" *li tov.* That is an actual *middah,* an actual emotion felt in the heart, connecting directly by saying, "*I* want." Here is movement from the state of pure intellect, which is totally removed from the world of emotions and from the state of understanding that it is important to have an actual feeling, to a very real down-to-earth feeling in the heart that motivates the person to act with feeling and emotion.

The first approach would be the pure *sechel,* intellect. In the second approach, when the *middah* ascends to the mind, the mind is superior and the emotions inferior. This does not lead to a result because what is primary here is intelligence. The mind recognizes a concept of closeness, or awe, or love, but it conceptualizes them without an actual *middah,* emotion. The third method is when the mind descends to the emotions and gives in and acknowledges the emotions as superior. I want it; I love it; I am completely identified with whatever the attribute is. This is an actual *middah* felt in the heart. However, this isn't the ultimate goal and perfection of healthy *middos*.

There is a more perfected approach that incorporates the first two methods mentioned in chapter 1, in the example of Efraim and Michoel. This ultimate goal allows each to retain their own identity. Chasidus takes this approach in making ideas and thoughts that are very lofty and delicate accessible to the average human mind without compromising an iota of their purity.

In the simple analogy, Ephraim and Michoel meet in the middle. One comes down the mountain halfway and the other goes up halfway, each person willing to unite with the other yet not being irresponsible by forsaking his true position. Imagine that Ephraim represents the mind, *sechel,* intelligence, and Michoel represents the *middos,* character attributes and emotions.

The first approach would be analogous to the *sechel* within the *middos,* the descent of the mind to the emotions. The second would be the elevation of the *middos* to the status of the mind known as *middos shebesechel.* The third approach allows for both, healthy concrete emotions felt in the heart, guided and harnessed by the intellect. The ultimate of the *sechel–middos* relationship would be the third approach. This is called *middos al pi sechel.*

In the first approach, when Ephraim goes down to Michoel, he is meeting him on Michoel's turf, saying in essence, "I surrender to you, Michoel. It's true that I am coming from above, but where I am going is below." What is primary, therefore, is that the emotions are superior and the mind is inferior; when the emotions are really in control, this is called *sechel shebemiddos,* intellect within the emotions. In the second approach, it is just the opposite; the emotions are elevated toward the mind, the *middos* within the *sechel,* or *middos shebesechel.* This approach actually has no relevance to daily life. It is the approach of the "absentminded professor," for the emotions are swimming in the ocean of intelligence, having nothing to do with the practical world. In the third approach, there is no superior and inferior. Both are true equals, each having its own unique qualities complementing the other, forming true unity.

The mind creates its own world, which is abstract and removed from the real issues of life, while the emotions are in the practical world. In the first approach we have emotions that are too strong, because the mind has given in to the immediate practicality of how we feel. In the second approach, we have the mind in total control and the emotions subordinate to the mind; therefore, when it comes to practical, real life there is nothing to relate to the world with. Our emotions and character attributes are simply reflections of the intellect. In the third approach the real practical world exists within a healthy framework, the clear and objective strength offered and given by the intellect. True feelings of love and awe for God must fall within this category.

Better understanding of how and why only the third approach succeeds in establishing true and heart-felt emotions will be facilitated by taking the emotion of *chesed* (loving-kindness) and analyzing it.

The Patriarch Abraham was the living embodiment of *chesed.* His kindness was magnificent and overflowing yet at all times guided by the objectivity of intellect. It happened that on the third day following his circumcision, when his pain was most severe, he left his tent to seek strangers to invite to his table so that he could feed them. How did he have the physical strength to go out of his bed? This ninety-nine-year-old man had just been inflicted with a wound and was in excruciating pain! This was possible because for Abraham it was a greater pain not to be able to be benevolent. While he was lying in bed he couldn't rest and be calm. His spiritual agony outweighed his physical pain, and he needed to find someone to help in order to achieve the peace of mind needed for recuperation.

The Talmud (*Sotah* 10:a) explains this verse in *Bereishit* 21:35: "And he called in the Name of God, Lord of the Universe," to mean that not only did he himself call to God but he made others do so as well. He always had people coming into his home to eat and drink. Having finished eating and drinking, they picked themselves up and were about to leave. He told them, "You have a choice: either give thanks to God for the food you ate or pay for your delicious meal," the price being a hefty sum. Of course they opted to thank God for the food. Let us delve into the details. It seems as though Abraham used blackmail to get his guests to do what he wanted! Can it be possible that Abraham was the true Jewish forefather when he used such tactics?! And finally, since Abraham epitomized the quality of *chesed,* to the point of putting aside his physical pain for the pleasure of helping people, then how is it possible that he would act cruel and mean? If this is the essence of Abraham, and it is, he didn't possess an iota of severity; so how could he say no, and pressure them, using harshness, which is the very opposite of loving-kindness?

Chasidus explains it by teaching us that true objective healthy emotions are guided by the intellect. This is

known as *middos al pi sechel,* in which there is the
unity of the intellect and emotions. An emotion is powerful and is felt in the heart. When emotions give rise to
actions, they do so with overwhelming power. This
causes a person to go too far and act indiscriminately,
in many respects to behave like an animal that acts
primarily based on instinct without discerning between
good and bad. Humans are not animals; primarily the
human modus operandi is intellect, which is cold, ana-
lytical, and rational, the complete opposite of emotions. How does a person bring these two worlds
together? It is by realizing that each has a place. It is the
responsibility of the intellect to tell what's right and
what's wrong. Once that's been established, the intellect calls upon the emotions to activate their warmth
and passion. Since the intellect realizes its limitations in
regard to acting emotionally, it therefore demands that
the emotions use their strength. This approach leads to
very proper and healthy emotions that are not out of
control. As soon as emotion wants to get carried away
in an improper way, it has a check–balance system,
called intellect, which prevents it from acting out of
line. Finally, both the intellect and the emotions are
activating their strengths and working in unison, each
desiring the other's assistance.

   In the case of Abraham, he had an obligation not to
allow the strangers to walk away without thanking God
for the food; that was his intellect harnessing his emotions. Yes, he does epitomize kindness. However, if he
had let them go, it would be Abraham's emotions acting
wildly, without intelligence. So on the contrary, because he was who he was is the very reason that he used
his intellect to intervene and guide his emotions. This
isn't blackmail; it's truth and wisdom.

Another simple down-to-earth example: a child plays with a knife, the parent takes it away, the child cries and is very upset. What's the parent doing, being kind or strict? The parent is in fact being very kind, but it is not an emotional, undiscriminating kindness, rather, it is true love because the parent is using the gift of the human species, intelligence, in fostering love and appreciation. The parent is activating a healthy emotion based on a healthy mind. This is the meaning of the *middos al pi sechel*.

What is the practical meaning of *middos shebesechel* and *sechel shebemiddot* in the *chesed*, loving-kindness, scenario? *Middos shebesechel* would be the realization of the mind that kindness and love are important. Therefore, the intellect has an intellectual bent toward closeness. However, it's all part of the mind and therefore the result is a subjective view of kindness based on the intellect. *Sechel shebemiddos* would be the justification of the mind in supporting the heart's desires. Here again the intellect is used as a pawn in supporting those emotional needs and therefore it is a very subjective view driven by the emotions. However, in the *middos al pi sechel* case, there is an objective view of *chesed*, since the *middos* are acting based on the intellect so that if the emotion goes too far and becomes overwhelming and subjective, along comes the intellect and says, "Wait a moment, that's not proper." This is true objectivity.

*Middos al pi sechel* and *middos* without the guidance of *sechel* can be compared to two contemporary ideas. The first is "tough love," which would be an expression of a *middah al pi sechel*. Yes, it's love; however, it comes through a tough approach. It takes the form of saying, "No, but I truly care for you and it's for your best interest that I don't give you what you want." The second would be "loving too much": expression of the emotion of love without even considering what kind of person the recipient is, just letting the emotions lead wherever they will. This approach can be very harmful to the character of an individual.

This objective approach, allowing the person his individuality yet being completely faithful to a higher truth, is one of the reasons the teachings of Chasidus incorporate the esoteric and unknown while yet communicating it through the exoteric and known. This enables a person to have the virtues of both and to have a very objective view of himself and the world around him.

# 3

# *Becheyn:*
# The Practical Result

### Terms

| | |
|---|---|
| *Choref u maksheh* | Sharp and challenging |
| *Musoon u masik* | Patient and conclusive |
| *Neshomah bloi guf* | Soul without Body |
| *Guf bloi Neshomah* | Body without soul |
| *Nigleh* | Revealed |
| *Nister* | Concealed |

This third approach is the unity between the mind and the emotions. It is analogous to Efraim coming down the mountain halfway and Michoel going up halfway, and they meet in the middle. Here emotions are controlled by the mind but not suspended in the medium of intellect. In practical terms, the mind is acknowledging there has to be a result, an impact on real life. The word being translated as "result" is *becheyn,* a word the Lubavitcher Rebbe always used, which means, basically, the bottom line. The result, the bottom line, is some

17

kind of human experience such as "*I* love God" or "*I* have awe for God." It's a result and feeling of the heart; yet at the same time, it is the kind of result that is governed and harnessed by the mind. It is a true synthesis. This may sound as though the mind is in control and in one respect that is true, as it says in *Tanya,* "the mind dominates the heart." But on the other hand the mind recognizes that the bottom line is that there has to be a positive effect on the world, and this can only be done through building character and emotional strength. A brilliant intellectual without good *middos,* good attributes, needs a lot of refinement.

One can find examples of this in personalities. In the legends of Torah sages, there was a famous Reb Zeyre who was called *choref umaksheh* (sharp) in his learning of Torah. Every day, he would spend a certain time learning and then ask himself twenty questions on what he learned. When he had answered those questions, he would go over the subject again to see if there were more he could ask. He was constantly refuting his own answers and revising his philosophies. Reb Masna, another sage, was known as *musun umasik,* patient and conclusive. Chasidus says that the difference between the two is that one was a great genius of the mind but never came to a conclusion because as soon as he had a conclusion; he refuted his own reasoning. Reb Masna was not superior in intelligence, nor was he a genius, but he was able to be conclusive and get to the bottom line. Chasidus says that the two are analogous to *halbashah* and *hafshotah*. Reb Zeyre, a genius of the mind, represented abstraction but was missing the bottom line, while Reb Masna had the virtue of the bottom line, of embodiment.

One more illustration from daily life: Chasidus teaches that there are three accounts that a person should make before going to sleep at night. One is, "What did I do today?" The second thought is "What could I have done?" To get up a half hour earlier would have made it possible to learn a little more Torah in the morning before work. If the person had truly wanted to speak to someone nicely at work, the person could have done it. The person can know who he is and what he can accomplish if he applies himself. The third thought is the ultimate truth: the activity that relates to the true purpose of creation, for example, a person could say to himself after reading the biography of a *tzaddik,* "I know that it is completely beyond me to treat every living creature with kindness. I can barely restrain my anger even toward people I consider my friends. But I know that this is the ultimate truth." Whatever the person's ultimate goal is, that's the third meditation.

Why is it important to have this third meditation? I learned from one of my Chasidus teachers that this meditation is the one that will result in growth from level to level. A push for growth comes from being aware of the ultimate truth.

By itself, the ultimate truth may not have much use; it is like a fantasy. This is comparable to *hafshotah,* abstraction. But as the previous Rebbe says, it has no result, there is no bottom line. On the other hand, if one focuses only on the practical accomplishments of today, this has no soul-essence in it. This would be like *halbashah,* embodiment alone, clothing and analogies and illustrations that never get to the point. When there is a combination of the two, there is a driving force to bring the ultimate truth of abstraction to the real world. This is the ultimate.

This concept can be compared to two other terms mentioned in the Talmud and Chasidus. They are *neshomah,* soul, and *guf,* body. In order for a person to survive, both are needed. In fact, without a proper combination of soul and body there will be a breakdown in the human mechanism. Could anyone operate only with the soul, negating health, sleep, and other bodily needs? That would lead to a deterioration of the person resulting in death, in which the soul ascends and cannot express its qualities in the practical world. The same is true if a person decides to function with the body only, disregarding the soul. Taking too much time in one's daily schedule for health and other important bodily needs, leaving no time left to allow the soul to operate in daily life, will also lead to a demise of one's true essence. Just as the body needs food, so too does the soul need its spiritual food. Not giving it its nourishment is improper and destructive. These two methods are called *neshomah bloi guf* and *guf bloi neshomah.* We find the same idea in regard to the study of *nigleh,* the revealed, exoteric part of Torah, and *nister,* the concealed, esoteric part of Torah. The Talmud would be part of *nigleh,* since its discussions center around tangible items such as marriages, holidays, food, and so on. The information contained is revealed and open to the human experience; therefore it is called *nigleh.* On the other hand, the Kabbalah is called *nister,* since its concepts are esoteric and abstract; a person's intellect is lost to its overwhelming lofty information. If a person decides to study *nister* only and not spend time on *nigleh,* this is incorrect. The feet must be firmly planted on the ground while the mind is ascending to the sky! Otherwise one can fly away and not really have an experience that's beneficial. Likewise, to study *nigleh* only without *nister* is tantamount to *guf bloi neshomah.* This would be similar to someone with his feet stuck in quicksand, unable to look up above, too occupied with what's below. In a contemporary idea, this would be analogous to being around negative people; one will notice that one's own statements and expressions will be negative, since all that is heard and seen is negativity, and that negativity is projected onto others. For this reason it's imperative to incorporate both the study of *nigleh* and *nister.* Of course, the study of *nister* must be understood as much as possible.

For this reason, Chasidus Chabad has developed a very systematic, organized study of esoteric concepts, yet at the very same time relating to it through the intellectual faculties, so that every person, regardless of his or her level of understanding of the pure abstract Kabbalah, can and should study *nister.* If one claims not to be ready to delve into *nister,* this is similar to saying, "I'm not ready to actualize my soul, I'll just operate with my body." This will lead to a very unfulfilled Jewish life-style. These two ideas are similar to the two basic tools through which God has instructed us: one, the study of Torah, and two, the performance of *mitzvos.* One without the other will not survive.

Thus the combination of *halbashah* (embodiment) and *hafshotah* (abstraction) results in wisdom that is totally beyond ordinary rational understanding, which at the same time is clarified through illustrations, parallels, and examples, in such a way that the depth of understanding is brought down to the real world without compromising its status. In this way, Chabad Chasidus does not compromise its modus operandi, which includes the depth of understanding of Torah and understanding of God. For this reason Chabad Chasidus can incorporate many teachings and thoughts of Kabbalah, which are totally abstract and esoteric, while at the very same time the sensible approach brings the mind down to the real world, where there is an actual understanding and feeling and emotion toward those ideas.

# II

# GOD'S MANIFESTATION IN THE PHYSICAL WORLD

# 4

# *Mimaleh* and *Sovev:*
# The Immanent and
# Transcendent Energies

**Terms**

| | |
|---|---|
| *Shefa* | Transmission of self |
| *Or* | Light |
| *Keli* | Vessel |
| *Giluy or* | Revealed light |
| *Or gunuz* | Concealed light |
| *Or makkif* | Peripheral light |
| *Or pnimi* | Permeating light |

It is posited in Kabbalah and Chasidus that Hashem has different ways by which He sustains the world. Hashem is infinite; thus it follows that His flow of energy is infinite as well. However, this world is finite, at least as compared to God's absolute infinity. Therefore, the infinity of Hashem's energy as expressed in this universe and in the world has different ways of manifesting itself. One of these is called *mimaleh kol almin:* the immanent and filling energy of God. It is given to the

25

world and impacts the world's creatures in a very personal and particular way.

The other flow of energy is called *sovev kol almin*—transcendent and encompassing. It enters the universe, but its impact is general and not particular or specific.

An analogy to *mimaleh kol almin* is the relationship between a *talmid* (student) and a *rav* (a teacher). The *rav* is way above the student in knowledge. How is it that the *rav* can communicate to the student? The *rav* has to do what we call a *tzimtzum,* meaning a contraction. He needs to contract his vast knowledge of the subject into a short and simple lesson so that he may be able to properly communicate knowledge to the student(s). If the *rav* does not contract his information, he overwhelms and confuses the student. The student, in turn, does not internalize anything because the *rav* is overwhelming his limited comprehension. He does not have the framework to which he can attach what seems to him to be a mass of disparate and contradictory ideas. In order for the *rav* to communicate, to teach the student properly, he needs to contract his intellect, which makes a difference in him. Before he contracted his intellect, the *rav's* mind was flowing with information without any contraction of intellect. Now he has pulled himself back in his mind to create space within his mind for the existence of a student. After he creates a place within his mind for the arena of a student or students, he now has to find methods to convey his information, because if the teacher contracts his intellect but does not find ways of expressing the contracted information, the student still will have nothing. Once the information reaches the student, the student reacts in a way conditioned by his own level of knowledge.

All these events and processes denote changes within the teacher and the student. The *rav* didn't have someone else in mind and now he has the student in mind. The *talmid* did not have the information and now he has the information. The reason there are changes is that when one is talking about communicating intellect, one is talking about giving over some information to an outside entity. There is a student; the student is separate from the teacher; what the student is receiving now is information. Even after the student receives the information, one can't say that the student is one with the information. Rather, the student has been given information, which he may or may not later integrate into his understanding and emotions.

This giving of information from teacher to student is analogous to what is called in Chasidus *shefah,* meaning a flow of energy in which there is a transmission of one's very essence to the recipient. This flow of energy is actual, not theoretical; the *rav* really is giving a piece of himself, vis-á-vis his information, to a student. The information comes to an entity, a separate existing being. Since that is the relationship here, it causes a change in the teacher and in the student as well. To put it another way, any time one gives of oneself to someone else, it is going to make an impact on both giver and recipient.

This concept of *mimaleh kol almin* is also known as an expression of God's *or pnimi,* the pervasive energy that fills the universe in an inward manner, permeating every creature. This emanation is limited and finite. Since creation and creatures are limited as far as how much they can absorb, if this energy were infinite it would overpower the minds and hearts of the recipients, causing total chaos and confusion.

However, in order for the finite world to relate and receive infinity, the infinite light must conceal itself. This is accomplished through the process of *tzimtzum,* contraction and minimization of the infinite, the result being *giluy or,* God's energy manifested in a revealed and open way to each and every person.

In regard to *sovev kol amin,* which Chasidus says is *makkif* because it is peripheral, what is being expressed is what we call the *or haganuz,* the infinite concealed light of Hashem. It remains infinite without contracting its essence. This is analogous to the master saying, "I want it to be this way," overpowering and overwhelming the individual, the servant. Chasidus says that the one drawback of *sovev kol amin* to *mimaleh kol almin* is comparable to a certain aspect of the servant–master relationship. The servant, from his perspective, doesn't really have anything tangible to walk away with because nothing was generated from within his psyche; rather, it came from outside, from his master. So as far as he is concerned, nothing has changed; he still possesses the feeling that being free from responsibilities is the essence and foundation of a good life-style. This the Talmud calls *avda b'hefkera nicha leh,* a servant likes to be free. Yet the servant follows his master's orders. Why? Or to take another example, one may go to a lecture where a genius is speaking and not know what he really said, but nevertheless recognize there is something unusual there and walk away moved. If someone approaches the listener after the lecture and asks what the genius said, the listener's response is, "I don't know, but it was unbelievable!" How is it that the listener can respond that way with confidence, when he can't repeat a word the genius said? Chasidus says this is an example of *sovev kol almin's* impact on the world. Just as the servant is moved to do what his master wants, even though from his perspective he resents working, so too does the infinite expression of God's energy cause all of creation to be moved in recognizing that there exists a God. Can it be explained, or proven? No; however it doesn't stop a person from doing what He wants. The person simply follows. So the very same overwhelming, forceful approach taken by the master is the impetus for the servant's obedience. So too in regard to the one drawback that *sovev* has in comparison to *mimaleh,* that drawback itself impacts the world. In other words, *sovev* is the infinite energy of Hashem impacting the world in a peripheral manner, and that is one of its strengths. On the other hand, the advantage of *mimaleh* is that God's infinite energy contracts itself in such a way, that what one feels and receives is based on the ability to handle and absorb it. So, from our perspective as human beings, we are the cause of God's revelation. This would be analogous to a person being able to communicate precisely what the lecturer said, not just a feeling of fascination. Therefore the manifestation of *mimaleh* is called *giluy or,* because it is *revealed* to us in a manner that we can appreciate, even though its infinity has been disguised to the point that humans only feel it in its finitude. Sometimes one might think that to have the *or hasovev* revelation in his or her life is a dream. However, I've met many people who weren't Torah scholars or great rabbis, and yet they had this sensation. When people met the Lubavitcher Rebbe, of blessed memory, at a *farbrengen* or some other occasion they walked away with this unique inspiration. Many of the people who came did not know Hebrew, Torah, or Chasidus; yet they walked out recognizing that the

Rebbe was a special man. What went on? Some would
call it intuition, or a special energy that he emanated. I
believe it was an expression of the *or hasovev*. Every
person has a conscious and a subconscious. Most function based on the conscious self, which is limited
within well-defined boundaries. However, there are
some people who are called *tzaddikim,* the very righteous, who have refined themselves to a point that every
fiber in their body is permeated with God's will. It is
these people who emanate an aura of the subconscious
in a revealed form. Simply put, anyone who meets them
perceives some magnetic force of Torah-true spirituality that draws others toward them. This is the infinite
light of the *tzaddik,* and that infinite light has an impact
on others. Impact is something that comes from outside. One can't internalize it because a human can't
internalize it. It is experienced as a fascination, a sense
of "Wow!" One can't internalize a "wow!" One can
only dwell on it and get excited. That experience is
*makkif,* peripheral, but its impact is immediate and
undeniable.

These two words, *mimaleh* and *sovev,* are analogous to another two words: *or,* or light, and *keli,* or
vessel. Chasidus spends much effort in elucidating the
relationship between light and the vessel. It is learned
from Kabbalah that the lights of Hashem gave energy to
the world (the vessels). In general, there are two ways
in which *or* and *keli* can relate to one another.

One is that the *keli* absorbs the *or.* In order for the
*keli* to absorb the *or,* the light cannot be overwhelming
or the vessel shatters. In the earlier example, if the *rav*
or teacher gives all his information to the students, the
students won't understand a thing and they will be
confused. So the *rav* must contract his *or.* When he

contracts his *or,* in what way is his *or* received by the student? Chasidus says that it is received in a *pnimius* way. This means that the student internalizes it.

*Mimaleh kol almin* is the energy of Hashem that is internalized by the world, by the creatures and all recipients. In order for this world to internalize it, it has to be limited. So Hashem takes His infinite light, and this expression of His infinite light vis-á-vis *mimaleh kol almin* is a limited light, so that the *keli* (recipient) will be able to handle it. The virtue of this style of manifestation is that the recipient can walk away with something because it is put in the realm of the recipient.

The second possible relationship between *or* and *keli* is that the *keli* experienced a change merely by being in the environment created by the *or.* The *or* is so much stronger than the *keli* that it is in another realm of being and thus does not destroy the vessel, yet its impact is felt, as in the example above.

This is the energy of *sovev kol almin.* Its advantage is that it provides a revelation of something higher than what the person can comprehend and take into himself.

There is a third level, which we will discuss in the coming chapters. This is *atzmus,* the essence of God.

To understand the relationship between *atzmus* and his *mitzvos,* let us examine the Chabad outreach approach. Why is it so important to these Chabadniks to run around Manhattan getting people to put on *tefillin?* Why are they so serious about encouraging the women at the local supermarket to light *Shabbos* candles?

At first glance it would seem that the performance of *mitzvos* only relates to Hashem as He is a Master, giving orders to his servants. This is the level of *sovev kol almin,* the godly energy that is infinite. He must command His people to do the *mitzvos,* because without His command no one would do them.

Does this mean that the Jew who does a *mitzvah* is only relating to something that Hashem has created, that is, this particular commandment, and not to Him as He is in essence?

Not so! The fascinating point of *mitzvos* is that to say *"Boruch Atoh Hashem"* is to connect to the very core and essence of Hashem, *"atzmus."* To understand this central point, we must first discuss the very highest powers of the soul.

# 5

# *Ratzon* and *Taanug:*
# Willpower and Delight

### Terms

*Hamshochas hanefesh*　　Drawing forth of the soul
*Kabbalas ol*　　The acceptance of God's yoke
*Adon*　　Master
*Eved*　　Servant

*Ratzon* means the will, but its real devotion is closer to what is meant by willpower, power of will. People often speak of willpower, but do they know how it operates? The will is not an independent entity outside the person who has the willpower. Willpower, or the will, is simply an extension of the self. The word for this in Hebrew is *hamshochas hanefesh,* the extension or drawing forth of the *nefesh,* the soul. In Yiddish, there is a word called *tzi* consisting of the letters *tzaddik* and *yud,* which means drawing forth, extending the self. The expression *"Ich tzi zich tsu dir,"* which translates as "I am attracted to you," literally means, "I extend myself to you."

33

Chasidus explains that when we are talking about the *ratzon* or will, we are talking about the soul, the *nefesh*. The *nefesh* is extending itself toward something else, toward what it wants. So will is clearly not an entity in itself but an expression of the soul. Take, for example, the students who are sitting in a class learning. Is it possible that two out of the class will understand the information identically? Yes, it is possible. The information is external, coming from outside, and it could conceivably be received by two people in the same way, each of them remembering the same parts. When two people take notes on a science lecture, where the information is very factual, often they write down identical things.

However, if two people have a want and a will to do something, is it possible for both to have the same will? Chasidus says no. It is possible to have an external will of sorts, where two people each say, "I like chocolate." But this is not will in the strong sense. In reality, each one goes about expressing will in a very different way, because will is an extension of the soul and all are different souls, unique and unlike anyone else. Will, in essence, touches the depth of the individual. Thus Chasidus spends a great deal of time explaining that it is really the willpower that is crucial in any decision. The will is the soul extending itself.

To explain this further, Chasidus draws an analogy between *adon* and *eved,* master and servant (or slave). What is the relationship between an *adon* and an *eved?* The premise of the relationship is that the servant is totally dedicated to the master. Whatever the master says, the slave does and follows, with no processing, debating, or challenging. This is what Chasidus calls *kabbalas ol,* the acceptance of the yoke of the master. "Yes, sir!" and no questions asked.

In this ideal relationship between servant and master, is the master doing something to the servant; is he coercing him? Absolutely not. Nor is he giving him intellectual reasons as to why the servant should listen to him. All he does is issue a command, a *tzivui,* and the slave listens and does what he is commanded.

Why? Because in this model the slave is essentially an extension of the master. The slave has a total commitment to his master. There is not a give-and-take; there is no change on the part of the master or any on the part of the servant. Since the servant conceives his identity as being an extension of that of the master, it is as if he doesn't exist as a separate entity, so no one has to exert effort. Deciding to do something with the right hand and then with the left does not involve explaining to the hands, or giving them separate instructions. As the Jerusalem Talmud says of *ahavas Yisroel,* love for one's fellow Jew, it is natural because all are parts of the same body. Similarly, the will is an extension of the soul, not a separate intellectual faculty with its own independent mental operations.

Let's go one step further, to another concept known as *taanug* or delight. According to Chasidus, *taanug* is even more powerful and more connected to the soul than will. How can this be? I just explained how the servant is an extension of the master. But the word *extension* means part of the whole, not the thing itself. Most simply: the servant is not called the master. The master has to say, "I want you to do this." Why does he have to say it? If they were truly one, he shouldn't have to say it. Even if we assume that when the servant sees himself in the mirror, he sees his master, still if the servant really were the master, he should be able to say, "I know what you want me to do because I know myself." But that is surely not the case. The master has to command the servant and if the master doesn't command, the servant doesn't know. The master has to extend himself. His extension is not to an outside independent being; it is to a being who is totally dedicated and committed to him, but it is still an extension.

This is what Chasidus says is the difference between *taanug* and *ratzon*. Granted the greatness of willpower still has a certain independence, on a very refined level. On the other hand, when we speak of pleasure, can it be explained in such a way that another person, even a dedicated servant, can become excited by that pleasure? Can someone understand why another has a pleasure in chocolate ice cream or a piece of Talmud? It can be hinted at in words, but it is not truly explainable in such a way that another person can participate in it, because it transcends intellect, will, and any form of expression.

Chapter 2 contained the example of Levi being drawn to Reuven and not Shimon. Both are just as intelligent and nice as the other. Why don't they evoke the identical response? The answer is, That's the way Levi feels. Is Reuven saying, "That's the way I want," or "That's the way I am"? The second is correct: delight *(taanug)* in comparison to *ratzon* expresses more of the soul's essence. A person can be made manifest through will, but in a deeper way a person is characterized by what his or her delights and pleasures are. If one analyzes people by the expressions of their will, one might be fooled. But one can never be fooled by looking at what a person delights in. Who a person is is a constant. Contemporary thinkers might say that it is impossible not to know who one is without engaging in denial, a purposeful disregard of the truth. And as the fourth Lubavitcher Rebbe says, "A fool only fools himself." He's not fooling God; he's not fooling others. He only fools himself.

# 6

## *Atzmus*:
## The Absolute Essence

### Terms
*Teva*    Nature
*Nissim*    Miracles

Having touched on *taanug,* the highest power of the soul, it is now possible to consider the concept of *atzmus. Taanug* is analogous to *atzmus,* the absolute essence.

In order to understand the concept of *atzmus,* it will be helpful to explain another idea. There are three concepts mentioned in Chasidus: (1) *teva* (nature); (2) *nissim,* the plural for *nes* (miracle); (3) *ein baal hanes makir b'niso:* the person to whom the miracle happened is called a master *(baal),* and the expression means, ''The master of the miracle does not recognize the miracle that has taken place.''

Let us first consider nature. What is nature? *Teva,* the Hebrew for nature, comes from the word *Tes, Bais,*

*Ayin,* meaning "to sink." Nature is the sinking of godliness. Godliness is submerged in the natural world, and God is not seen. I look at the table and Hashem is not apparent. The same goes for other aspects of nature. Yet at the same time, all aspects of nature have their source in godliness and express some aspect of godliness, inspired and directed from *mimaleh kol almin,* the light of Hashem that fills all matter in an internal way, specific to the individual entity.

This is analogous to the relationship between the rabbi and the student. When the rabbi teaches, every student gets the information that he can handle, because the student relates in a certain way. Similarly, regarding nature, Hashem is present in it. But Hashem has imbued Himself in nature in such a way that one can say godliness is particular to every aspect of nature.

Second, there are miracles, which are basically the shattering of convention, like the splitting of the Red Sea. Miracles are an expression of God's unlimited energy, known as *sovev kol almin.* This expression of energy is analogous to the will. The will is that aspect of the self that says, "I want this. I don't care how it was yesterday; I want it now, today. Don't give me any excuses, any rules or regulations!" When the willpower operates, nothing can stop it. Think of the child who wants something and won't take no for an answer. Why? Because the willpower is all-powerful and awesome; it's like a bulldozer that will roll over anything in its way and uproot anything on the ground regardless of the object's weight or size. Likewise, *sovev kol almin* is the energy of Hashem that shatters the laws of convention. A miracle is an obvious expression of *sovev kol almin,* one that enables people to see in their lives or in the world collectively the inexorable will of Hashem.

However, they don't understand it. They don't have the words to explain it in a rational manner. The only thing that can be said is that it comes from God. This would be analogous to the parable mentioned in the Talmud. A thief has just finished breaking his way into a house. As he is about to go inside, he asks God to help him be successful! How is this possible? God is the one who instructs him in the Ten Commandments not to steal, yet he somehow doesn't follow and steals anyway. However, before he does so he wants God to be on his side! A paradox! Chasidus says no, he isn't crazy; rather, it's quite normal. He prays to God because he has faith in God; faith can be peripheral and therefore it doesn't really touch him to the point where he actually changes his behavior.

The faith of this robber, being *makkif,* or peripheral, impacts him—he relies upon it to achieve his urgent desire. However, he has failed to integrate it into his rational self. Had he meditated on God's benevolence and on His ethical demands, he would realize that Hashem must have in store an honest way for him to make a living.

The concept of *atzmus* means the Absolute God. This is the third concept: the master, the person to whom the miracle has happened, does not realize that the miracle has happened. To wake up in the morning capable of walking and talking, that's a miracle. Few people are even aware that it's a miracle to breathe and walk.

That's why there are prayers of thanks to Hashem upon awakening and prayers of thanks to Hashem for going to the bathroom. Because, God forbid, if one of a person's orifices closed up, that person would be in trouble. The *baal hanes* doesn't even realize and recognize that this is a miracle.

The existence of miracles that are not even recognizable to the one they happen to, says Chasidus, doesn't come just from the encompassing light of Hashem. This actually comes from the very core and essence of Hashem known as *atzmus*. Why? Because this is so deep that it does not express itself in a premeditated fashion. The way that it expresses itself is through living life. Breathing doesn't have to be thought about; it comes naturally. This absolute essence of God is so completely disguised that people aren't even aware of it.

The truth of the matter is that Hashem transcends all manifestations and all revelations, whether they be open and revealed miracles or the natural forces all around, because no one can say merely that Hashem is just a natural God, nor can anyone say precisely that He is only a supernatural God. Either way would be putting a limit on God. The ancient philosophers said that Hashem is so great, He enjoys His activity with the supernal worlds—implying, but not with humans; humans are too low. But Chasidus says that would be heresy! Why? Because such a statement limits Hashem to being a super-duper God. Is that what Hashem is? If Hashem can only be a super-duper God, an Almighty God, and He can't be a simple God, then He is limited. At the same time, if He is only a simple God, then that too is a limitation.

Then what is Hashem? Hashem is Hashem, as in the first words of the Ten Commandments: *"Anochi Hashem Elokecha."*—I AM. What are you? Chasidus explains that before God expresses Himself as Hashem, which is the most holy name of God, the Ineffable Tetragrammaton, and before He manifests himself as Elokecha, the name of God associated with nature, He says that He is, *Anochi*—I AM. Not Hashem, not the *Yud K Vov K,* not Elokim and Elokecha, meaning your God, referring to Elokim the name whose numerical value is 86, the same numerical value as *teva,* nature. All those are limitations. I AM. ANOCHI. Chasidus says: *"Anochi asher Anochi—*I AM WHO I AM.'' GOD IS. God is the experience of living life without any premeditated notions of His divinity. So when the question is asked, "Who are you, God?" the answer is, "Just look around you. I'm everything you have and everything you relate to. In other words, I'm so much part of your life that I'm disguised within you and your environment, yet at that very same time and place I'm with you.'' So, when He wants to He makes Himself sensible and understood; He puts Himself into nature or miracles, and when He doesn't, He does not. And to show that the essence of Hashem transcends, He says, "I AM.'' This is analogous to the concept of *ein baal hanes makir b'niso.*

That is *taanug,* what is known as delight. No one can really describe their pleasure or make anyone else feel it because pleasure is not tangible. It can be described in words, but it is not felt in the same way. One person can say to another, "I love chocolate ice cream, I love reading Talmud,'' and so on, but the other person doesn't have any true feeling of the first one's pleasure; all he knows is a mechanical description of what the first told him. Why is he not able to communicate his pleasure? Why does another have a different pleasure? Because pleasure is not describable. It is identical to the concept of essence—*atzmus*—which absolutely transcends the rational and is part of a person's essential makeup. So asking why pleasure can't be communicated is analogous to asking why two people weren't created exactly alike. That is one of the beauties of God's creation: each and every one is different. As the contemporary saying goes, variety creates beauty.

# III

# PURPOSE AND DESIRE
# OF CREATION

# 7

# *Dirah BiTachtonim:*
# A Home for God
# in This World

**Terms:**

| | |
|---|---|
| *Nisaveh* | A spiritual "lust" |
| *Mitzad tachtonim* | Generated from man's perspective |
| *Ah lichtiker dirah* | A bright and illuminated home |
| *Etzem* | Essence |
| *Kol etzem biltei mischalek* | Every essence is indivisible |
| *Kol etzem biltei mispashet* | Every essence is nonextensible |
| *Giluim* | Manifestations |
| *Mah* | God's holy name, whose numerical equivalent is forty-five |

An important term to understand is *dirah bitachtonim,*
which means making a dwelling place, a house for God
on earth, just as a person has a home. The Midrash says
that God had a desire to have a home and He desired to

have his home here, not anywhere else. This is eluci-
dated in the *Tanya* on the basis of a saying found in the
*Midrash Tanchumah*. The Alter Rebbe (the first Lubavitcher Rebbe) explains that *nisaveh haKodesh Boruch Hu lihyos lo dirah bitachtonim,* meaning God
desired to have an abode on earth, refers specifically to
this mundane and corporeal world. He explains that the
higher worlds discussed in Kabbalah are all spiritual.
They are worlds of revelation, but the essence of God
cannot be grasped through spiritual revelation. It will
be shown that this material world, as a place of spiritual
darkness, is the place where God's essence can dwell.

The word *nisaveh* in this context needs interpretation. The normal word used in the Hebrew language
meaning "want" is *ratzah*. Therefore, when describing
God's desire for creation, seemingly the more appropriate word might be *"ratzah HaKodesh Boruch . . ."*
Chasidus explains that the choice of the word *nisaveh*
and not *ratzah* not only communicates the purpose of
creation, which is the what in creation, but also the
who involved in creation.

To understand this, it will help to mention some
reasons for creation. In the Kabbalah there are several
reasons mentioned why God created the world. One
reason is that, since God's nature is good, therefore it is
natural for the good to do good. For example, a person
who is truly good won't be able to function unless he or
she is performing acts of loving-kindness. This type of
an individual will seek out others to help. Following
this logic, God, being naturally good, seeks something
to bestow His goodness upon. Hence He made the
mundane world. Chasidus doesn't accept this as a final
reason for creation, because God transcends nature,
God acts in supernatural ways when He so desires. So to

say God's nature is good is a limitation on God's true infinity. Just as in the example, a person who is compelled by his nature, even though he does great benevolent acts, yet this very virtue of character limits him to always being good. There are times when this same person needs to be strict and severe, and yet he isn't able to free himself from his ''good'' nature. In contemporary terms, he can't say no. The same follows regarding God. To say God's nature is good is tantamount to saying God is limited and forced to act in a certain way, and that simply isn't true. When He so desires, God manifests Himself in what we call good, and when He desires to act in a manner that we perceive as strict, that is His choice. It is for this reason that Chasidus rejects this explanation as the ultimate purpose for creation. God could just as easily have created the world in such a way that His action would be based on His supernatural qualities, which aren't necessarily limited to projecting goodness in the format adapted to our way of life and understanding of the universe.

Another reason mentioned in the Kabbalah for creation is that God wanted someone to appreciate His creation. Therefore, He created the physical mundane world with people being the subjects. Again here Chasidus doesn't accept this as the *ultimate* reason for creation because the heavenly realms that were created appreciate His greatness much more than we do. This world is full of *klipah*—negative energy—and the wicked prosper. Here a human must struggle to appreciate God and face many tests on a daily basis just to control human passions. So why would God in His infinite wisdom create a world that conceals Him? This refutation is alluded to in the section of the Tanya mentioned earlier. The Alter Rebbe says that since these spiritual worlds are a descent and digression in comparison to God's essence, they aren't the ultimate reason for creation. I heard another way of explaining these words. Since there are always other lower worlds below those spiritual realms, the spiritual realms aren't the ultimate reason for creation, otherwise why did God create something "lower" and more coarse than the spiritual refined levels? Based on this interpretation, the meaning of "since they are a descent" means that there is a descent and something even lower. If this is the case, it is obvious that God desired something lower, and in fact He desired the lowest of the low! Therefore Chasidus says that God's desire to have someone to appreciate His creation is not the ultimate reason. So what is the ultimate reason for creation?

The answer is, there is no answer. To understand this requires focus on the exact language used in the Midrash Tanchumah. The word *nisaveh* comes from the Hebrew word *taivah,* meaning a desire beyond rational. In modern culture it would be called a lust. The word *lust* has a negative connotation. However, the Hebrew word *taivah,* means a strong desire that impacts the person in such a way that nothing else does. Simply put, when a person has a *taivah* for a certain thing, he doesn't use his rational power of judgment at all. If something smells or tastes good, he wants it. He will do anything and everything to get his *taivahs*. The same is true in regard to God creating the world. God had a *taivah* to create the world. He didn't allow anything to get in His way, including those rational reasons mentioned earlier. Therefore, when the question is asked, "why did He need this materialistic world?" the answer is, God had a positive spiritual lust! As the Alter Rebbe put it, *"Uf a taivah, iz nit kein kashah"*: When you have a spiritual lust, there's no question. Desire transcends questioning.

The Alter Rebbe explained as follows: *"Uf a taivah iz nit kein kashah"*: Regarding a *taivah,* a spiritual desire, there is no question. Why? Because when we talk about Hashem's lust to create the world (the word *taivah* is used in the Midrash), there is no why. God creates the why and the answers. It's an oxymoron, a contradictory expression. If Hashem is omnipotent, then to say that Hashem has to give an answer is limiting God to questions and answers—to the realm of rationality, which God transcends by definition. Hashem can certainly ask questions and give answers whenever He wants; but to say that humans must be given a why is limiting, and it contradicts the idea that Hashem can create anything. Such a limited God would not be the God of the Torah. This would be the who involved with creation. Since the reason for creation comes from God, who is beyond human reasoning, therefore the part of God involved in creation is the true absolute essence of God. It is similar to a person who has a particular *taivah*. Stop and ask him where is it coming from, and he won't be able to give you an answer, because the *taivah* comes from a place within the person that transcends questions and answers. It comes from the essence of the individual.

Ultimately God does transcend "why" and therefore no one can ask "why." However, another question can be asked: not why did He desire creation but what was His spiritual lust? The Alter Rebbe answers that the spiritual lust was to have a home, *bitachtonim*—in the lowest of all worlds. The expression used in Chasidus for this idea is *dirah bitachtonim. Tachtonim* literally means lower, and *dirah* means a house. When we use

the expression *Dirah bitachtonim,* we are referring to
a home in a place that is the lowest of the low. This
word expresses two ideas: (1) the *dirah* should be in the
*tachtonim*—He wanted it *in* the lower worlds; (2) He
wants this *dirah* to be generated by the world as world.
This is known in Hebrew as *mitzad tachtonim, from
the perspective of* the lower world. What does this
mean? An example can be drawn from the story of how
God took the Jews out of Egypt on Pesach. The Midrash
says that many of the Jews in Egypt were immersed in
idol worship. Basically, the truth is that they weren't
worthy of being redeemed. Hashem says, ''You're my
people. The fifteenth of *Nisan,* out you go!'' But the
people say, ''We have idols in our backyard. Where are
we going?'' Hashem knows what He's doing and says,
''You'd better run out of Egypt and leave everything
alone.''

The Jewish ancestors were not strong in belief in
the one God. This was the nature of the redemption of
*yetzias mitzraim,* the Exodus from Egypt. This redemption and revelation were not from their perspective but rather were from the perspective of Hashem,
which essentially takes over and gives power. However,
as soon as He takes away His *ko'ach,* His power, the
person to whom power was given will go back to being
the same. The next day after going out of Egypt, everyone was still the same person as before.

Not until the forty-nine days of traveling to Mount
Sinai did anything happen. Those days, known as
*Sefirat HaOmer,* are symbolic of the transformation
that comes from gaining a new perspective generated
from within a person's character. This, Chasidus says,
would be the concept of *mitzad tachtonim,* from
''our'' perspective.

Another example: A student goes to a class, takes notes, hears everything that is being said, and understands it. But it's not him. It's not where he's coming from; it's not who he is. That is, it does not come from his perspective. It comes from the teacher explaining the concepts; he understands them but it's not him. It's not *mitzad tachtonim*. He has been fed information, he has all the data, but he doesn't live it; it's additional information being stored in his mind. So even though it would be considered *Bitachtonim,* yet it was initiated by something outside of his true self. Why is it important from God's perspective that the motivation come from him?

Chasidus explains this with an analogy. A king is a king in his palace because his palace is entirely expressive of his true essence. This can be true of every person, but it is made clearer by thinking of a personage like a king. A king in his palace is at home; he can be dressed or undressed, can wear any garments, and can act any way he wants. On the other hand, the king when appearing in public expresses himself in royal garments, in a kind of disguise. The king's essence is expressed in the palace. This concept is known as *etzem,* the essence. God wants His home to be a place where He can express His essence. The only way this is possible is if the home itself is made out of essence material. It would be inappropriate to have a king dwell in an old broken-down shed in the middle of the woods. Why? because it's not respectful for a king and for what he represents. The same logic would apply to the Jewish people's mission in making a home for God. If the home isn't generated by living people in this material world, but rather by God's initiative, this is tantamount to having an old broken home for the king in the middle of the woods, because the inhabitants of this world haven't done anything for God but have remained in the old self, complacent and self-centered. What God wanted in creating the world was to be appreciated from the human perspective. He wanted each person's essence to be there for Him. He wanted a transformation of human character. This transformation would be the only true way of welcoming Him into the house, the Jewish essence greeting the divine essence.

This concept is also known as *ah lichtidiker dirah,* an illuminated, bright home. There are two parts to a home. One is the house itself, its rooms, walls, ceiling, and so on. The second is the furniture, lights, and all other items that make the bare walls beautiful. What is the spiritual parallel? What do we learn from the idea that Hashem has some kind of home that is dark and bare and from the fact that the same home is then lit up? This is the concept of *ah lichtiker dirah, lichtik* meaning bright and illuminated. A person can be in a home that's dark and filthy, living there and having some form of existence. However, existence in that environment will cramp and confine his very spirit. On the other hand, if the home is beautifully painted and decorated in the latest fashion, this will create an entirely different type of existence for this individual, because this well-lit and bright home is truly the place where his essence manifests itself. In the moral realm the same is true. God says, I want a bright, illuminated home. Surely I can also dwell in a dark home; however, in order for you and I to realize and appreciate this relationship, you need to make your home manifestly godly. Saying God is all-present and all-powerful is true. However, if it remains in words and doesn't express itself in action, it is considered a dark home. God would say, I don't feel at home! This is why it is God's will that the *dirah* be made in a manner that's expressive of God's essence and the human's essence.

Since we've mentioned the concept of essence, let's broaden our horizon by elucidating the details that are an integral aspect of the essence. Chasidus says, "If an essence is in its essence state, then it is completely essence throughout." Chasidus uses two concepts to clarify this: (1) *kol etzem biltei mischalek*—every essence is not divisible. If an essence is not divisible, then it's an entity, it's complete; (2) *kol etzem biltei mispashet*—every essence does not extend itself.

What does it mean that an essence is not divisible? A person whose modus operandi is truth and essence will be truthful everywhere. Not only will he behave this way in a proper environment that corresponds to his beliefs and life-style or at work where his coworkers are observing him, but also in places that are distant from his way of living and thinking, where no one sees him and he can do whatever he so desires. There, too, will he activate his essence and not be swayed by those foreign forces. He is who he is; there is no difference. So, this essence is true all over. Even if he is in a place that seems to act under a different sense of rules from his, he is not affected, because he is expressing, living, walking, and breathing his essence. This essence is indivisible. He doesn't say, "I left that part of my essence back home; now that I'm away from my community I'll act with that part of me that wants to behave in ways that are contrary to my real true self." This is not a person connecting to his essence; essence cannot be divided, it is either true or false all the time. Put in other words, a person's essence is an absolute nonderivative and noncomposite state of being that is fundamental to his or her very existence.

What does it mean that an essence doesn't extend itself? Do we not find the person who is truthful in various places? It would seem that his truthful character in each place is an extension of his essential truthfulness. But in fact, the change of situation does not affect the essence; the entire essence is with him. If a person has extended himself he has concealed his essence, and not all of his personality is functioning in the same way it usually does. That would not be an essence.

The extension could, however, be what in Chasidus is called a *gilui,* a manifestation and revelation. (In speaking of God Himself, the concept of *gilui* is often mentioned in Chasidus in connection with *or*-light. This is called *gilui or,* meaning a revelation coming from a place within God that has contracted [i.e., hidden] His essence and is only vivifying the world with His extension.) The concept of *giluim* is used to refer to creation, in the sense of an external manifestation that is affected by the world.

To give a practical example, there are times when a person may take into consideration what people will say about his or her religious behavior. After all, since humans were created on this planet, humans are affected by it. People dress a certain way based on what other people are saying. It's quite possible that deep down they are very uncomfortable with their wavering frenzies. Since Jews truthfully know who they are, they have a right and an obligation to say to themselves, "Enough with this pleasing others; it's time to please the Creator, God Almighty." These two attitudes would be examples of an extension and essence. The first reaction is analogous to the concept of extension, since it extends the true self and goes outside of what one is really all about. On the other hand, the second response is similar to the concept of essence, since it responds with truth coming from the person's essence, which doesn't care what people will say: all that's important is what God says.

For this reason Chasidus explains the concept developed in Kabbalah that Moshe Rabbeinu was a *"neshamah* of *mah,* a soul [of a level of godliness] coming from *mah." Mah* is one of God's holy names. Its numerical equivalent is forty-five. This godly name retains its identity wherever it is. Therefore our sages teach us that Moshe Rabbeinu was born three months premature. Chasidus says the reason is that Moshe Rabbeinu was so pure that he retained his purity even though he did not have the last three months of pregnancy to protect him. Moshe was a soul so unaffected by the world that he did not need that additional refinement. He was pure in the level of *mah,* whose numerical value is forty-five *(mem-heh),* like the name of Hashem that equals forty-five, symbolizing the purity and pristine state of the essence throughout. This is analogous to the idea that a state of essence is indivisible and nonextensible.

# IV

# THE THREE DRIVES
# WITHIN THE HUMAN

# 8

# *Nefesh Habahamis:*
# Natural Animal Soul

## Terms

| | |
|---|---|
| *Neshomah* | Soul |
| *Ko'ach ha'misaveh* | Power of passion |

Chasidus explains that there are three souls: (1) *nefesh habahamis,* the animal soul, also called *nefesh hachiunis,* the vital soul or natural soul; (2) *nefesh hasichlis,* the human rational soul; and (3) *nefesh ha'elokis,* the godly soul. The third aspect of the soul is unique to Jews; Gentiles have both an animal soul and a human rational soul.

To understand the significance of the three souls, one must first understand what a soul is. It means, basically, a drive. A soul is something spiritual or not of the body. The Hebrew word used for soul is generally *neshomah,* but in operating terms it means a drive, a direction in which a person is moved. After describing each soul in a general way, the discussion will move on to understand each in more detail.

61

The animal soul, the *nefesh habahamis,* is similar to an animal in that it desires animal-like pleasures. It does not use its intellect to discern between good and bad; similar to an animal that acts based on its instincts, its intellect is subordinate to and overpowered by what it sees and feels. Notwithstanding this fact, the animal does possess a drive of passion, which makes it unique and different in a positive way, in distinction to all other species of creation. The passion that the animal has can be used for many positive and constructive tasks, such as plowing fields or transporting people, and sometimes it even teaches us humans what is proper and what is improper. The Talmud explains the advantage gained by having an ox plow a field, the result being an abundance of wheat. If a human being were pulling the plow, the amount of wheat harvested would be minimal. When animals shlep a wagon with people as passengers, it will get to its destination much quicker than if that same wagon were pulled by real live people. When it comes to performing hard chores, people get tired and hungry much more quickly than animals, and give up doing the task.

We also learn wonderful lessons in values from animals. Take for example the incident mentioned in the Torah of Billam's donkey. She basically scorned Billam for acting out of order and hitting her. Of course the ability for a human to understand an animal's language is miraculous. But animals do have their own language, and part of that language includes a silent message. It is a language that teaches ethics and goodness, just as it taught Billam a very important lesson. The Talmud says were it not for the Torah prohibiting stealing, that prohibition could be derived from a cat. A cat doesn't steal food, even though the food lies around

and is open for grabs, as long as it feels it might belong
to another cat. In the written Torah, the Prophet Isaiya
scolds the Jewish people by saying, "The ox knows its
master, the donkey knows the crib of its owner, however, my nation [Israel] doesn't know Me [God]. . . ."
This statement clearly demonstrates the goodness and
obedience with which animals listen and follow, and
the verse also teaches how humans should behave and
learn from them. If I had to sum up an animal's special
quality, I would say it is "passionate determination."
The animal will do anything and everything to get what
it wants or to get what its master desires; nothing can
get in its way. All of these qualities are found in the
animal soul.

The animal soul in its very essence is neutral, not
evil. But it is passionate; it is full of desire. The direction
of its desires, the way its passion will be directed, de-
pend on its environment. An analogy would be the air all
creatures breathe. The function of the lungs is to breathe,
but the type of air taken in depends on the environment.
Whether in the smog of Los Angeles or the fresh air of
the countryside, the lungs will still do their work, but
what ends up in the body will be very different. Likewise with the animal soul: in a materialistic environment
of money and physical pleasure, this soul will desire
material things; in a bad spiritual environment where
God, Torah, and *mitzvos* are concealed, or worse,
scoffed at, the drive will be harnessed in the paths that
lead to spiritual corruption. However, in a good spiritual
environment, one of metaphysical beings and angels or
simply good and decent God-fearing people, its passion
will be directed toward spiritual godly things. Imagine a
puppet; the movements of the puppeteer's hands deter-
mine the direction the puppet follows.

The same is true for the animal drive. Chasidus teaches that the *nefesh habahamis* is able to connect more passionately with God than the *nefesh ha'elokis!* The reason, as we will see later, is that the strength of the *nefesh ha'elokis* is *elokus*—godliness—which necessitates a more calculated approach than the simple passion used by the *nefesh habahamis*. Therefore, the passion for God as seen from the *nefesh ha'elokis's* perspective is limited. This is similar to the person who's been eating nonkosher food for years and all of a sudden decides to do *teshuvah,* return to God, and stop eating food that a Jew shouldn't be eating. He then starts doing more *mitzvos* and following the Torah. This person's fervor and enthusiasm is totally passionate for God, literally, he is in love with God! To compare his practice of *mitzvos* to people who were born into a family that never saw, smelled, or knew what nonkosher food looks, tastes, or smells like is to find that their practice of *mitzvos* is dry and cold—it is missing a heart and soul. Why is it this way? Because when something is natural to a person it doesn't mean as much compared to something that's new and unnatural to a person's experience. So since the *nefesh habahamis's* desire for God is a novelty, it is passionate and constantly fresh, warm, and exciting. On the other hand, the godly drive, since its desire for God is natural, doesn't get excited about godliness. On the contrary, it says, "What's the big deal; I've been having this experience for many years—give me a break!" Subsequently, its passion for God is not there. This special quality is called the *ko'ach ha'misaveh* of the *nefesh habahamis,* the power of passion.

# 9
# *Nefesh Hasichlis:*
# The Rational Drive

### Terms

| | |
|---|---|
| *Yesh mei'ayin* | Something from nothing |
| *Milmato limailo* | From below to above |
| *Milmailo limato* | From above to below |
| *Isarusa d'leilu* and *d'litato* | The arousal from God and from us |
| *Teshuvah* | Return |
| *Bichirah* | Free choice |

The drive of the human rational soul, the *nefesh hasichlis,* is intelligent and logical. Its purpose is to figure things out. This soul looks for cause and effect, system and organization, clarity. It will perform this function wherever it is. Since the *nefesh hasichlis* is found in the domain of intelligence, which is part and parcel of the very fiber and makeup of this physical world, it feels at home when focusing on worldly matters. It allows itself to become the intellectual tool for the animal drive.

They share something in common in that they both begin their operative system from a this-world perspective. Therefore they naturally use each other to coexist. In actual practice, the animal soul tries to get the rational soul to serve its needs, to use its logical and rational capacity to figure out how to accomplish its desires and fulfill its passions. The rational soul also engages in justification and rationalization of those desires.

Chasidus explains this concept by taking the idea of creation ex nihilo, known as *yesh mei'ayin,* and showing us the approach of the *nefesh ha'elokis* and the *nefesh hasichlis* toward it. We know God created the world. He as the Creator is infinite. He chose to contract His infinite power in order for there to be the creation of a limited finite universe. This process is known as the *tzimtzum.* The created universe is called, *yesh,* meaning "something" and God, as the Creator, is called *ayin,* meaning "nothing." What this means is that prior to the contraction of the infinite power, all that existed was something that is totally beyond rational human experience, namely, infinity. Therefore, from a human perspective it's nothing—*ayin*—a human can't know what it is, it's not tangible or real in the earthly domain, therefore to a human it is "nothing." On the other hand, what God did create is very tangible and real. A person is able to identify with it and say, "I know what this is; it looks this way and it feels a particular way." Therefore it is called a "something"—*yesh.*

Chasidus continues to clarify this point. The outlook of the *nefesh hasichlis* on all aspects of form and matter is *m'yesh l'ayin,* meaning from the "something" to the "nothing" conclusion. The process of analysis used by the *nefesh hasichlis* in understanding and relating to all physical and material matter is, first and foremost, accepting the fact that the physical item really exists and is here in the real world. It draws this conclusion since the "*yesh*-something" can be seen and felt. On the other hand, the cause of how it got here is not seen and felt; therefore, from the *nefesh hasichlis's* perspective it's not here, it's *ayin*—nothing, it has no worldly existence in that it's not tangible. Chasidus calls this process of analysis *milmato limailo,* from below (the worldly tangible vantage point) to above (the heavenly abstract view).

The *nefesh ha'elokis,* on the other hand, views all physical and material matter and form from just the opposite vantage point, *mei'ayin liyesh,* from nothing to something. Its primary interest is the *ayin*—God—who is called "nothing" since He is unknown. From there the *nefesh ha'elokis* comes to the conclusion that there is a something that is the result of the *ayin's* doing. He calls it something because from its perspective it's merely a "something," the fact that it's here and functions as an entity having very little significance and importance. The *nefesh ha'elokis* begins its relationship with matter and form by first and foremost finding out how the matter and form were created, who made it, and why it is here. This is called *milmailo limato,* from above to below.

So to recap, the two opposite approaches used by the *nefesh hasichlis* and the *nefesh ha'elokis* are: (1) the rational response is primarily interested in the effect and its ancillary interest is where it came from; and (2) the godly response is primarily interested in the cause and how it got here; the fact that it's here is a mere by-product and result.

There are two other terms that are used as synonyms. They are *isarusa d'leilu,* an arousal from (above) God, and *isarusa d'litato,* an arousal generated by (below) man. To help understand these terms, here is a practical example. Several years ago a fellow popped into our *yeshivah.* I approached him and asked, "How did you get here?" He said he was fleeing from someone who was trying to hurt him, so he got into his car and drove from Nevada to California. As he was driving, he noticed a synagogue. He parked his car and came into the *shul.* The rabbi approached him and asked him if he needed any help. He told the rabbi his story. The rabbi immediately brought him to the *yeshivah* to begin refining his life through finding out his own roots. He never had the opportunity to study Torah and was raised in a very non-Jewish manner.

As I reflected on his story, I realized that his return to Torah was what Chasidus calls *isarusa d'leilu.* Why? Because prior to driving down the road in California, he had absolutely no idea and interest about Judaism, and yet hours later he found himself in the *yeshivah!* Amazing. How is it possible to make a 180-degree turn in such a short period of time? The answer is, it comes from God; it is not human doing. Rather, God intervenes in a person's life and provides an awakening and arousal called *teshuvah*—return. This imparts the ability to make a complete change in life-style regardless of the fact that the mental, emotional, and spiritual states of being are not even in the realm of returning to God. This is why this *isarusa d'leilu,* the arousal that one feels to make a move, is generated by God, *d'leila* from God, who is above. This is also the meaning of *milmailo limato,* from above to below.

The second set of terms expressing the opposite approach, is *isarusa d'litato* and *milmato limailo.* To clarify, every year, a month before the Days of Awe,

Jews prepare themselves by taking stock of what tran-
spired in their lives throughout the previous year. Just
as every businessperson knows the importance of taking inventory at least once a year, so do the Jewish
people. The Holy Days are a time of judgment, a serious
and awesome time, requiring reflection and taking inventory of what actions from the past year need improvement and how to implement an organized plan to
avoid going through the same difficulties.

This approach of self-reflection and meditation
is also known as *teshuvah*. However, it is completely
different and the opposite from the *teshuvah* approach
mentioned earlier. This *teshuvah* approach is generated from within; it is initiated from within not inspired by other people or a holy environment, such as
a *yeshivah*. This is called *isarusa d'litato,* referring
to the person who is *limato* (below), meaning here
on earth, which is called "below," in comparison
to *limailo* (above), which is called "above," referring
to God, who is above, beyond the earthly mundane
experience.

In other words, the *isarusa d'litato* approach is
coming from within. It is very calculated and thought
out, but the *isarusa d'leilu* approach is coming from
God, and since God is infinite, its effect cannot be
foreseen or estimated before it happens. That's why it
doesn't have to take time to adjust and prepare to go
from a wilderness empty of Jewish knowledge to the
peak of the Jewish experience, the *yeshivah!* Since it is
not internally generated one simply allows oneself to
be swept away with the current, landing wherever God
wants in order to get one's life back on track.

Another very important dimension and quality that
is unique to the *nefesh hasichlis* is the issue of *bichirah,*

free choice. When we say a Jew has the freedom to
exercise his or her will to do what's right or what's
wrong, which part of the Jew are we talking about? The
part of the Jew that wants to be godly and Jewish, the
*nefesh ha'elokis,* is preset and "forced" to act in a
Jewish way because the only language and life it knows is
Judaism. Therefore, from its perspective there is no true
choice in doing God's will. The *nefesh habahamis* is
also predetermined as far as its choice. It desires the
mundane and corporeal, since that is its modus operandi. So it too is "forced" to act like an animal; therefore, it doesn't have true free will. When it is said a Jew
has free will, what is being addressed is his *nefesh hasichlis,* his rational mind, which is impartial as to any
particular practical and emotional behavior. The *nefesh
hasichlis* is *sechel,* intelligence. It has the capacity to
make a true choice that is free from any preconceived
notions of what is right and what is wrong.

We see here that a struggle is going on—what the
*Tanya* calls the "battle over a city." The godly soul tries
to get the rational soul to rise above the world, while
the animal soul tries to get it to justify its desires and
lusts. What is at stake here? What is the aim of this
battle? To conquer the human rational soul. The human
rational soul is where free choice exists. The intelligence can come to appreciate that there is something
beyond, or it can choose to justify the animal soul's
desires, which say that the body and material things are
more important. This is the general picture: the battle
between the godly soul and the animal soul to dominate
the rational soul.

It can now be understood that a Jew's primary
"job" is to harness the *nefesh hasichlis* in a direction
that is godly and Jewish. Chabad Chasidus provides the

tools and information to properly accomplish this very important task. Therefore Chasidus Chabad incorporates the human mind in relating to God, for it is the mind that is of key importance in really and truly being a servant of God. If the mind lacks commitment, even though the godly soul is on fire with the love of God, the person, as a rational human being living in this world, is not in love with Him.

# 10

## *Nefesh Ha'elokis:* The Godlike Response

### Terms

*Pintele Yid, Nikudas haYahadus*   Quintessence aspect of a Jew

*Chelek eloka mimaal mamash*   An actual part of God

*Malach*   An angel

*Klipas Nogah*   Translucent force

*Sholosh Klipas Hatimeios*   The world of defiance

*Elokus shenaaseh Nivreh*   Godliness that becomes part of creation

*Ratzah*   Yearning

*Shuv*   Retreat

The *nefesh ha'elokis*, or godly soul, is the true Jewish essence, the *pintele Yid*, and it is directly connected to God, literally a part of God. Since it is godly, it is not limited; it transcends the ordinary material world. From the perspective of the rational and animal soul,

73

indulgence in worldly pleasures could be justified. But the divine soul tells us there is something beyond, a true godly spirituality. It says, "If something in this world does not manifest God, it is not for a Jew, because it is contrary to his or her real essence."

To understand this in a deeper way requires asking several questions. What is the significance of the *nefesh ha'elokis* being a "*chelek eloka mimaal mamash*," an actual part of God? Also, do righteous gentiles posses a *nefesh ha'elokis*? If not, why not? Just because they aren't born to a Jewish mother and have not had a proper Jewish conversion, why should this exclude them from attaining the same union as Jews have? Also, what is the highest spiritual level a gentile can reach?

Chasidus explains that the *nefesh ha'elokis* is actually part and parcel of God. It manifests itself by the very fact that a Jew cannot and will not be able to forsake his or her Jewishness. Regardless of circumstances, every Jew possesses a godly soul, even though temporarily the Jew might drift into strange nongodly pastures. This fact has been demonstrated many times. I myself have witnessed hundreds and hundreds of people who have been far from Judaism, and after their godly soul was rekindled they revealed their inherent relationship with God. How is this possible? If one is not mentally or emotionally cognizant of God, what is the stimulus that causes the search for one's roots? The answer is the *neshomah*, the godly soul. This soul has never been lost, because it not only comes from God but is actually a part of God. Therefore, just as God transcends time and space, the same is true in regard to everything that is part of Him. As the Baal Shem Tov says, "When you grab part of Him, you're actually holding on to all of Him." God is inseparable;

He is God all over and at every time. The only reason it is said that God has placed part of Himself within the Jewish soul, which indicates at first glance a departure from the essence of God, is that verbal expression, is limited, whether it be Hebrew or English; therefore, there is no other way of conveying the concept that the *neshomah* is totally united with Him without saying *chelek eloka mimal mamesh*, the godly soul is an actual part of God, mentioning clearly God having a part to Him. However, this "part" only enhances His powerfulness—it expresses His omnipotence and His true infinity.

Based on these ideas, it becomes possible to understand the spirituality of a gentile. A gentile is not a Jew. The very fact that a gentile is born to a non-Jewish mother establishes this fact. This in no way denotes inferiority but rather a different method of fulfilling his mission in life. Therefore, even a supremely righteous gentile doesn't have a Jewish soul known as a godly soul, a *neshomah*. What does a gentile have? Chasidus develops a kabbalistic concept to help answer this question. This is *klipas nogah*, the translucent husk. There are two kinds of coverings upon a light. One type is so thick, no one can see through. The other type of covering lets through a certain amount of light; it conceals the essence but the appearance of the object is still visible. These two coverings are analogous to the two types of negative energies that exist in the world. There is what's known as *klipas nogah*, which corresponds to the see-through type of a curtain, and there is *sholosh klipos hatimeios*, meaning the completely negative forces that preside within the universe. The type of curtain that totally conceals what is beneath it, corresponds to this type of *klipah*.

A righteous gentile's soul comes from *klipas nogah*. This means that he possesses a level of spirituality that expresses some revelation of God. He lives by the basic idea that God is good and that His desire of humankind is to make the world a better place, a place in which all of society has the proper tools, including modern technology, to accomplish this task. When a gentile assists in this mission, he attains and expresses his soul and is called a righteous gentile, the reward being, as Maimonides says, that he will receive a portion in the world to come. However, a gentile doesn't have a *nefesh ha'elokis* and doesn't have the same responsibilities as a Jew does. Therefore, a gentile isn't able to connect to that level of God called essence. An example of this would be a father who has two children; one is a teacher and the other is a plumber. Does he see them as better and worse or does he appreciate each in the role he plays? True, there is a real difference, but it doesn't make one good and the other bad. The same holds for Jew and gentile.

Chasidus takes this one step further. The difference between a Jew and a gentile can be compared to the difference between a *neshomah*-soul and an angel. An angel is limited to its mission. Whether it is kindness or severity, an angel cannot go beyond whatever role God has placed on that particular angel. Michoel, the angel of *chesed* (loving-kindness) is limited to kindness. Gabriel, the angel of fire and severity, is limited to destruction and cannot do acts of kindness. Therefore, in the Torah there is an episode in which God sends three different angels to accomplish three different missions. Why didn't God have one angel do all three? All three missions were in close proximity to each other. Are angels some kind of limited physical beings, limited to a certain place?

The explanation is that angels are spiritually limited to the functions given to them by God. They don't have the free will to do whatever they want. That's why God assigned three angels. The three tasks necessitated three different spiritual approaches. On the other hand, a *neshomah* is limitless. It can be kind and at the same time strict. On the contrary, if a *neshomah* isn't able to do all kinds of spiritual missions that involve kindness, judgment, and compassion, then the *neshomah* isn't doing its job. Based on this explanation, *neshomos* are called *mihalchim*, walkers, and angels are called *omdim*, standing. An angel in comparison to a soul is standing in one place based on its particular mission. On the other hand, a *neshomah* is constantly going and walking from one mission to another. This activity of a *neshomah* includes totally opposite missions. Therefore, *neshomos* are called "walkers."

In the same vein, we can explain the difference between the soul of a Jew and the soul of a gentile. A gentile is limited to his or her mission. That's the way God created him or her. Therefore, the level of spirituality for a gentile is limited to perfecting himself and the world around him. Yet a gentile cannot transform himself to become limitless. He is a creation of God, just as all other creations. Therefore, there is a defined application to his ability. This is called in Chasidus *givul*, limited. However, a Jew is not a creation of God, rather a "part" of God; therefore a Jew is able to go beyond the boundaries imposed by nature. The reason is, a Jew is not a creation of God, rather a Jew is godliness as He expresses Himself in creation through a *neshomah*. This concept is called in Chasidus *Elokus shenaaseh nivreh*.

We now understand the term *chelek eloka mimaal* in a deeper way. However, what still begs clarification is the term *mamash*, meaning actuality. Of course the *neshomah*, being a part of God, is actually that. If so, what is meant by *mamash*?

Chasidus points out that the word *mamash* comes from the word *mamoshes*, meaning tangibility. This means it can be touched with hands. If this is the case, how is this possible, when the *neshomah* is not tangible? So, Chasidus says, no! The *neshomah* is tangible in that it allows itself to be seen and felt by means of its association with the physical material world. Basically, when a *neshomah* activates itself and permeates the physical matter of the body, it then becomes tangible through the material. So one who touches the material that has been impacted is actually *mamash*, touching God! This is the significance of the *neshomah* being a *chelek Eloka mimaal mamash*. On one hand the *neshomah* is godliness, the epitome of spirituality; on the other hand the *neshomah* enclothes itself in the material corporeal form that conceals God. This is called in Chasidus *ko'ach hamafli lasos*, the wondrous power of God, in that God has put Himself in the physical material world. This is a great miracle!

This concept was addressed by Rabbi Sholom Ber of Lubavitch, the fifth Lubavitcher Rebbe. When asked to explain the seemingly contradictory terms, *mimaal* and *mamash*, he responded by saying, "It's the idea of *ratza* and *shuv*." *Ratza* means the desire and yearning for godliness and *shuv* means the retreat and return to the physical world. Chasidus elaborates on this concept and gives several examples to understand it. One of these examples is the talmudic story in which four rabbis have an experience in which their souls ascend to *Pardes*, meaning the Garden of Eden or Paradise, and three out of the four simply can't handle the divine revelation. The fourth rabbi is Rabbi Akiva. He, the Talmud says, "entered with peace and departed with peace."

The question raised by the Lubavitcher Rebbe is, "Why does the Talmud say he entered with peace?" It would suffice to say he exited in a peaceful manner in contrast to the other three rabbis, one of whom didn't exit at all, while the other two exited as disturbed and broken men. The Rebbe answers that the reason Rabbi Akiva was able to leave in a peaceful way, even though he had just had a completely transcendent experience, is that he entered in a peaceful manner. If Rabbi Akiva had not made up his mind prior to entering that he was going in "with peace," then he too would have never made it out in a normal fashion, the same as his contemporaries.

What is the concept of "peace"? *Shalom*, or peace, simply means there are two entities that cannot exist together because of their contradictory natures, and all of a sudden a third entity enables them to be able to make peace and agree with each other. Rabbi Akiva realized that the material world of *gashmius*, physicality, is a contradiction to the *Pardes*, which is a world of *ruchnius*, spirituality. How was he going to make peace between them? He realized it would only be by bearing in mind, prior to entering the Garden, that there is a higher power than both the spiritual *Pardes* and the physical world. This is the true essence of God, who created both, and He desired to bring harmony between them. On the contrary, from God's perspective, if there is a blockage between the two, then He, God, is not being expressed at all. *Pardes* doesn't express Him without incorporating the physical reality.

This is the meaning of Rabbi Akiva entering with peace, and only because he came to this realization did he succeed in exiting properly. His friends all entered with a desire to forsake the material world. Their ambition was to "space out" and have a *ratzu* experience. Finally, after so many years of learning about this great Paradise, they now had the opportunity to run away from it all and never come back! This had been their yearning and longing! Not so Rabbi Akiva. He kept in mind the true purpose of creation, which is the *shuv*, the return to the common human reality. This, he realized, was the zenith of godliness, not remaining in a state of spirituality unassociated any longer with the physical; on the contrary, the true purpose of creation is to work on having the spiritual permeate the material.

In chasidic terminology this would be known as *shuv sheb'eratzu*, the realization of the purpose of creation within the desirous state of cleaving to God. It's not enough to say, "I'll have a feeling of love and ecstasy *now*, and I'll forget about everything around me; all I care about is being with God. Later, I'll deal with the real world." The reason this isn't a proper attitude is that there might never be a later; it might be too late. A person must think about the reason for creation at the very beginning, even prior to getting involved in the burning desire to be absorbed by God. Otherwise, if he allows himself to have this experience, there won't be the opportunity to "come back down" to planet Earth!

To make this more practical, imagine the initial relationship between a man and a woman. If one partner intends only to give and doesn't have in mind, at the time of their initial contact, to restrain himself and draw the line and say no, this relationship is going to be doomed. It's not adequate to say, "I'll hold myself back later, once we are married; now I'll give my entire self

without any boundaries.'' Free and true love is based on
a disciplined, organized approach, as discussed in the
chapter on *sechel* and *middos*.

Now, a better understanding of how *mimaal
mamash* can go together becomes possible. The entire
purpose of *mimaal* is *mamash*. If a person just desires
the state of *mimaal*, this is the *ratzu* state mentioned
earlier. If a person wants only *mamash*, this is the *shuv*
state, which also isn't the purpose of creation. What is
necessary is the realization that the purpose of rising
*mimaal* is to refine that which is *mamash* in order to
reveal the godliness hidden within it; and that both go
together. We could say this would be called ''the
*mamash* within the *mimaal*.''

# 11

# The Intellectual and Emotional Components of the Three Souls

### Terms

| | |
|---|---|
| *Oved* | An active servant of God |
| *Tikkun* | Mending |

There are more subtle dimensions to these three drives. This is explained in a letter of the previous Lubavitcher Rebbe. In this letter he reminds his readers that the whole purpose of the spiritual journey, according to Chasidus, is to change one's naturalness, to alter the very nature of one's character. That is to say, whatever is natural to a person—even though it may be very good and beautiful—requires being changed, being elevated to a higher level.

The Alter Rebbe says that not only the *middos raos*—bad—but also the innate Jewish *middos tovos*—good, including benevolence and compassion—come from the *nefesh habahamis* and *klipas nogah*! That seems to be a radical view. After all, imagine having a tremendous love to help others, so much as to actually give away most of one's time, money, and energy, just to help another person. One might think this is the greatest form of self-sacrifice. Yet according to Chasidus, if it is natural to act in this manner and it doesn't demand any real sacrifice since it comes so naturally, then this action is *klipah*. Chasidus doesn't see this as a radical perspective, rather as the essence of Torah observance. To do the most holy and godly act is great. However, if the motivation and inspiration is based on a purely natural response, without a positive struggle within to overcome inner obstacles to giving, then this holy activity is ego-based and is therefore *klipah*.

This means that, from a certain perspective, nature is negative. This does not mean it is evil, but it can be a weight or an obstacle that prevents one from growing and developing spiritually. For example, if it is easy for a certain person to give charity, then that person may become self-satisfied and not question whether the giving springs from the correct motives. Such a person could give thousands of dollars and yet, from a chasidic perspective, nothing has been accomplished. (Of course, this is speaking not in terms of *halachah*, which specifies how much a person should give and what the limits would be, but in terms of promoting spiritual growth.) The expression *maaseh ha'tzedakah*, usually translated "the act of giving charity," can also be interpreted as "to *force* (one) to give to charity," based on the word *m'asin*, which means to force. Likewise with learning: if it is easy to sit and study six hours a day, and if one doesn't push oneself to study an extra fifteen minutes, then one isn't becoming in this area a "servant of God," an *oved Hashem*.

We find this concept in the Talmud. In the era of the Talmud, it was the custom to repeat Torah studies one hundred times. The Talmud says that if a scholar repeated his studies just one more time, one hundred and one times, he was given the title *oved Elokim,* a servant of God. On the other hand, if he were to repeat his studies only one hundred times, he would not be considered a servant of God! Why would the one extra time put him in this category? The reason is based on the previous discussion: the hundred and first time is an indication that the first hundred times as well were done out of a deep commitment to God, which went beyond the person's nature. The proof is the fact that he repeated his studies more than called for by tradition. This is indeed the lesson hinted at in the first chapter of the *Tanya.*

Chasidus uses the term *oved,* with a *vav,* rather than *eved,* without a *vav,* to emphasize the present tense: each person must be constantly reassessing whether he or she is growing. If I am the same today as I was yesterday, I'm nothing. This seems to be a radical position, a slap in the face of every good Jew. Yet it is not intended as a put-down. Chasidus is telling us, ''Don't be big with your Torah or your good deeds. Don't become complacent and self-satisfied, saying, 'I studied this much and I gave this much, so I can pat myself on the back.' ''

On the other hand, this is not intended to be taken to an extreme, motivating anyone to cause himself physical or emotional torture or pain. The point is to go beyond what is natural and easy, to feel the struggle, to persevere through difficulty.

With this in mind, the previous Rebbe explains the dynamics of the three souls. Each of the three souls

mentioned in the foregoing contains its full complement
of intellectual and emotional components. The Rebbe
explains that the animal soul, which is naturally directed
to the material, has an intellectual component that reasons according to its own understanding, which is concerned with self-preservation and self-justification. The
emotional component of the animal soul is what is
called the *yetzer hara,* the evil inclination. That is to
say, the intellectual part of the animal soul is the means
of *planning* and *justifying* the act; the emotional part
of the animal drive is the *inclination* to do evil. At first,
it might seem that the goal should be to break the
desires of the evil inclination. But, the Rebbe says, true
service is not in breaking them but in fixing them.

In other words, there are two types of service: to
subjugate and to transform. To subjugate one's desires is
simply to refuse to listen to them, to ignore them: "Just
say no!" to the *yetzer hara.* This would be, for example, to discipline oneself always to refuse to eat nonkosher food, to refuse the cheeseburger. A higher level
of service, however, is to transform that desire, so that
one only wants kosher food, to be completely satisfied
with that food, and to eat with a godly intent, with the
same degree of pleasure.

This obviously takes some work. The previous
Rebbe explains that the service of mending and fixing,
what is called *tikkun,* begins with the intellectual
attributes of the human rational soul. Part of *tikkun*
is to engage in the study of Chasidus. This includes
the contemplation of ideas, according to one's level
of understanding: how Hashem created the world, the
purpose of existence. It includes the study of *tefillah,
davening,* what we communicate to Hashem in our
prayers. These studies have an impact on the heart.

Eventually, with His help, we will have a different set of desires.

The reason the mending process begins with the rational soul and not the animal soul is that the natural drive cannot relate to meditations and contemplations that are God-oriented. Its modus operandi is acting like an animal and getting its passionate desires fulfilled. This is a stubbornly emotional approach. Talking sense and logic goes contrary to its desires; it won't pay attention. For this reason a person can only begin the process of *tikkun* with that part of his character that is in the realm of logic and consistency. This is the rational soul. That's also why the mending process doesn't begin with the godly soul. Since the *nefesh ha'elokis* is naturally in love with God, it doesn't relate to a possibility of not obeying God's will. Therefore the *nefesh ha'elokis* doesn't understand why he should take of his valuable time and energy and devote it to the *nefesh habahamis*. In other words, the *nefesh ha'elokis* and the *nefesh habahamis* are at opposite extremes—there is a schism between them. To bring them together requires an intermediary, this intermediary being the human rational drive. It can speak and understand both of their languages. Therefore, it can and does make peace between them.

The emotional attributes of the intellectual soul, and of the divine soul as well, are called the *middos*. The intellectual soul has an emotional side that tends to be drawn to what is below it. Since it is in a material world, it faces this world and directs its energy to what is directly before it. It naturally tends to focus on figuring out what is here and how it works. The divine soul, on the other hand, is drawn to what is above it, what is beyond the ordinary world. The Jew's task is to change the *middos* of both these souls.

On the side of the human rational soul, it is important to recognize that one should turn to the good not because it is rational but because it is God's commandment. Although one may think he is a basically good person, the reality is that he is doing what is "good" because he understands it. Only when rationality goes beyond itself and places God first is there real change in the nature of this soul. Then the human rational soul goes beyond its natural limitations.

This change of nature within the rational soul isn't just an interesting project. Rather, it is of vital importance to the very existence of the Jew. The reason is, there are many gentiles who do good because it's the proper thing, it's etiquette, or it's the custom of a particular environment. However, the world has seen in the past seventy years how more than a few differing peoples and nations have rationalized and justified murder in the name of goodness and fairness. The nation that was known as the intellectual leader of the world destroyed millions of people. How could that have happened? Weren't they the most intelligent nation? Weren't they the most sophisticated? The answer, is they were limited to intellect, and that was the reason they indeed did murder. They justified their behavior; they felt it was a good thing to kill. It is only when intellect goes beyond its own capacities and realizes that there is something more important than itself, namely, God, that it becomes possible to put aside one's own intellectual nature and truly do good. It's only this approach that provides an objective view of what is good and what is wrong. Otherwise any individual's view is subjective and tainted.

On the side of the divine soul, the *middos* want to be absorbed in God. As mentioned previously, the true desire of the *nefesh ha'elokis* is to have a *ratzu* without a *shuv*. However, the Jew's job here is to redirect this longing toward the physical world by transforming the material into the spiritual. That is to say, the divine soul wants to leave the body, leave behind corporeality and materiality. But God put the Jewish people here in order to transform that energy as well, to aim not only at spirituality but also at bringing a higher energy into the world. Each Jew can and must remain in the physical world and still be a godly person.

Why is it that Chasidus instructs Jews to change the very nature of their character by refining the *nefesh hasichlis* and the *nefesh ha'elokis?* Why not work on changing the nature of the *nefesh habahamis?* The reason is that change necessitates a willingness to listen and follow. If a person doesn't allow himself to try a change in his life, he will never have any perception that there even exists another approach. It is only after a person is open to saying "I might be wrong," or "I need to look for another alternative," that the potential for change can be actualized.

Therefore, since the *nefesh habahamis* is totally consumed with its desires and passions, it isn't able to begin thinking that it might be on the wrong track. All it can see is what it wants and it uses its intellectual component to get it. On the other hand, the *nefesh hasichlis* and the *nefesh ha'elokis* are open enough to realize that there are other approaches and therefore are willing to try a different approach. It's because of this openness that Chasidus recommends dealing with the *nefesh ha'elokis* and *sichlis* and not the *nefesh habahamis*. In other words, no one can change without becoming aware that there is something wrong with his current life-style. The *nefesh habahamis* doesn't have any clue that something might be wrong. The *nefesh hasichlis* and *elokis* at least have an idea that the natural approach to things is not the ultimate. Therefore they are willing to examine themselves and to make changes.

This is the reason the third Lubavitcher Rebbe, the Tzemach Tzedek, said that this idea is the very heart and soul of Chasidus. To stop and think rationally about this concept is to realize that the teachings of Chasidus are nothing less than the key to growth and development as people, and particularly as Jews.

These are wondrous and beautiful concepts, fascinating to contemplate. To think about these ideas is to gain great clarity about one's identity and activities.

# V

# SERVICE OF GOD WITH *KOCHOS HANEFESH*, SOUL POWERS

# 12

# *Chochmah, Binah,* and *Daas:* Concept, Comprehension, and Concentration

**Terms**

| | |
|---|---|
| *Chochmah* | Concept |
| *Binah* | Comprehension |
| *Daas* | Concentration |
| *Chesed* | Loving-kindness |
| *Gevurah* | Severity |
| *Tiferes* | Compassion |
| *Netzach* | Endurance |
| *Hod* | Adoration |
| *Yesod* | Bonding |
| *Malchus* | Royalty |

Chasidus emphasizes the refinement of character through meditation on ideas that are way beyond daily mundane affairs. The purpose for such an approach is the necessity to be totally removed from the ordinary day-to-day mode of thinking. Interestingly enough, this approach is used daily. Millions of dollars each year are spent on vacations and retreats to places were it is quiet, serene, and peaceful. People spend money they earned in an earnest way and put in a bank account just for the purpose of taking that desired vacation. Why? Because they desire to rethink their values and the purpose of their life and their relationships. In order to success-fully accomplish this goal, one needs to be removed from the daily hustle-bustle. So people get away, far away. Chasidus teaches that in order to accomplish this task, people need to remove themselves daily, in the midst of the chaos. The way to do this is through meditation. Within Jewish meditation there are all kinds of practices and forms; therefore Chasidus recommends certain basic information as a preliminary tool to be able to properly meditate.

Chasidus demonstrates the power of a total re-moval from daily affairs at least during one's prayer. The impact can be enormous, affecting the rest of the day. These meditative thoughts must incorporate expe-rience, yet transcend it. If the meditation is abstract only, a person won't relate and connect. Subsequently the meditation will pass as a wind without the person being moved to a change of character and values. For this reason Chasidus suggests combining both the ab-stract concepts mentioned in the Kabbalah and the down-to-earth issues. These earthly matters begin with the self, the way a person is made, who he is, and what are his experiences. Chasidus constantly quotes the saying mentioned in the prophet, ''From my flesh I perceive godliness,'' meaning the better a person un-derstands his ''flesh,'' that is, himself, the better he can understand God.

One of the most commonly used thoughts to sup-port the previous ideas is the notion of the ten *sefiros,* realms of godly expression. God has developed and chosen ten different ways in which He expresses Himself. He isn't limited by these paths. Rather, He uses their strengths and positive messages as a vessel to filter His essence through in such a manner that can be effective. These very same ten realms are found within every person's being. Here the discussion will focus on the ten human soul-powers and leave their spiritual counterparts, the ten supernal *sefiros* for you to study in the *Tanya,* and particularly in a treatise called *Mystical Concepts in Chassidism* by Rabbi Dr. Jacob Immanuel Schochet, printed at the back of the bilingual edition of the *Tanya.*

The first character trait is called *Chochmah,* literally meaning *wisdom.* However, a better translation would be *concept.* Take, for example, when a person is sitting and thinking about a certain mathematical query. Hours go by and finally she comes up with a brilliant idea that can be used as an invention. This is what is called *Chochmah.* It's the flash of an idea that is the creative force within the human experience. However, if the person were asked what happened, how did she suddenly figure it out? What is it that created the thought that supports this invention? She would say, "I don't know"! Why? Because the experience of *chochmah* is a flash. She hasn't yet developed the tools of the mind to answer all the questions; all she knows is that something clicked. What it is, she can't tell. This is what is meant when a person is called a *chocham,* having the ability to be creative.

It's only by experiencing this concept stage that what follows is *Binah,* understanding and comprehension. This would mean, using the previous example, when the person continues to think about the idea and goes one step further, to develop the idea with her mind by comparing it to other similar ideas that she has studied, this leads to a thorough comprehension of the flash. Now she can tell you the hows, whats, and whys involved with this concept. Now the idea has left the stage of concept and entered the arena of development, allowing the human mind to have the proper words and explanations to talk about it in a rational, intelligent way.

This is the talent of a true maven, a word derived from the root word *binah.* To be a maven is a specialty and a skill that very few possess. The reason is that to be able to take an abstract removed concept that has no body, no hands, no feet, entirely formless, and somehow to develop it to the point of understanding it in a clear logical fashion is an amazing task that only someone who is a maven can achieve. To understand an existing well-explained and developed thought doesn't make one a maven; many people do that in their personal and business lives.

Yet even after the *binah* state, there is something of key importance still lacking, which therefore necessitates a further process known as *Daas* or *Daat,* concentration. When a person develops an idea to the point of fully understanding it, what happens often is it remains in the realm of an intellectual concept. It is understood, it can be explained, it can even be communicated to others, but it's missing life! It's not *the person.* When does it become part of the person, when it is internalized by concentrating on the developed idea. As mentioned in the Tanya, chapter 3, the word *daas* is associated with the word *yoda,* meaning concentrated knowledge. The Alter Rebbe explains that when Adam had relations with Eve, the Torah expresses itself by saying, "and Adam knew Eve." Initially it seems very strange to use the word knew to mean cohabitation, yet the Torah does indeed use this word. So the Alter Rebbe explains that the only way to have a desired result from a union is through an effective concentrated bond. This only comes when the male concentrates on the female; otherwise, as the Talmud elaborates, there would not be any lasting result. True, both Adam and Eve would have had a pleasant experience, but no part of their true selves would have been passed on in the form of offspring.

Using this as an example to understand the term *daas,* what follows is the transformation that *daas* works on the developed idea. It now moves from the state of being pleasant intellectually, to the state of it being a part of the person. Now the person has it; before *it* had the person. *Daas* means concentration; to concentrate means to focus so that nothing distracts. It is this very powerful tool of *daas* that facilitates a quantum leap for the true refinement of character. This is the reason the Kabbalah calls *daas maftecha d'kolil shis,* meaning a key that includes all six, the six referring to the six emotional traits. *Daas* is the intermediary that bridges the gap between the world of *sechel* and the world of *middos.* The two are on opposite sides and it takes a special quality to bring them together. *Daas* provides that. *Daas* understands that in order for the intellect to succeed in getting its message across to the person, it is necessary to incorporate the emotions, otherwise the intellect will remain in a world of its own, separate from reality. This is now *daas,* which includes the six *middos.*

Since *daas* is an intermediary between *sechel* and *middos,* it must have part of each within it. Otherwise it could not affect both. For example, think of a mediator. He needs to take into account both sides and opinions. Otherwise he will fail in the negotiations, causing a total breakdown between the parties. The mediator has to put himself in the shoes of both parties, not only intellectually, but also emotionally, so that he should truly understand them and represent them both fairly. Of course this has to be done with caution and in an objective manner, guided by the intellect, as we discussed in the chapter dealing with *middos al pi sechel.*

The same logic is true in regard to *daas. Daas* not only bridges the gap between the two worlds of intellect and emotions, but it also incorporates both within itself. It completely comprehends the intellectual concept and is able to discuss it, yet it also has within itself a component that realizes the bottom line is a refined character and an emotional state that's healthy.

This also adds insight into the chasidic adage that the first and foremost quality that a *chasid* needs is *daas,* common sense. *Chasidim* resented fools, in the sense of being foolish in simple down-to-earth matters. This is supported by a saying I once heard at a chasidic get-together. The Chabad custom in regard to the exact language used in the *siddur* (prayer book) is that the first blessing said after the three standard blessings in the *amidah* (the eighteen blessings recited thrice daily) is *atah chonen liadam daas,* "You have given man *daas,*" keen perceptive knowledge. In other Siddurim-prayer books they say, "You have given man *binah* and *haskel,*" understanding and wisdom. What can we learn from this language in the Chabad prayer book? So this *chasid* explained that in Chabad, what is most important is *daas,* simple common sense, not *chochmah* or *binah.* And that's why someone who was a fool needed to change that part of himself before really connecting with the Lubavitcher *chasidim.*

This isn't a form of arrogance, rather a realization that *daas* is what makes a person. To concentrate means to be focused and thoughtful. This is at the heart of Chabad Chasidus. Other chasidic groups use their emotions as their central focus to serve God. The result is that they go about their own life similarly focused on emotion. On the other hand, the Lubavitcher *chasid* uses *daas* as the focal point. Without *daas,* the Chabad *chasid* is lacking proper form. Ultimately the person who achieves *daas* will be a stronger, healthier character guided by concentrated common sense.

# 13

## *Chesed, Gevurah,* and *Tiferes:* Loving-kindness, Severe Restraint, and Compassion

### Terms

*Chabad*    An acronym for *chochmah, binah,* and *daas*

*Pnimius* and *Chitzonius hanefesh*    The internal and external aspects of the *nefesh*

*Shem Elokim*    The name of God meaning judgment and strength

*Gevuras geshomim*    Very strong rainfall

*Tiferes ola ad ein sof*    *Tiferes* ascends to the infinite

*Chagas*    An acronym for *chesed, gevurah,* and *tiferes*

The terms *kochos hanefesh, chochmah, binah,* and *daas* are also known by their acronym, Chabad, the "Ch" alluding to *chochmah,* the "B" to *binah,* and the "D" to *daas.* They are also called *pnimiut hanefesh,* the inner aspect of the soul. They are called "inner" because they stimulate the external expressions of the *nefesh,* which are the six *middos,* beginning with *chesed.* For example, children have very petty emotive traits, getting upset easily when their desires aren't met. This is because the intellectual components governing their minds are immature and undeveloped. In other words, their perception (*daas*) of what is important and significant is infantile.

Since the intellectual aspect of the *nefesh* is more removed from the outside influences in comparison to the *middos,* which are more impacted by the *chitzonius,* the external, therefore we say that Chabad of the *nefesh* is *pnimius,* they are "closer" and more internal to the *nefesh.* The *middos,* whose function is to relate emotionally to the world around us, are necessarily influenced by that world. Intellect, whose strength is the ability to remove itself from the world and survey it dispassionately, is much closer to the true interests of the *nefesh.*

The *middos* of the *kochos hanefesh* begin with *chesed,* loving-kindness. *Chesed* is the willingness to diffuse kindness to everyone without discrimination. In Kabbalah it is mentioned that there are two kinds of *chesed,* that of Avrohom and that of Yishmoel. The *chesed* of Yishmoel is called *chesed* of *klipah,* which is negative. The *chesed* of Avrohom is *chesed* of *kedushah,* holiness, which is positive.

Chasidus explains the difference. Both Avrohom and Yishmoel were very kind and giving, but the giving of Avrohom was based on self-nullification. He felt that other people were just as entitled to his physical and spiritual possessions as he was, since these were a gift from God. Yishmoel, on the other hand, experienced a feeling of self-aggrandizement from his possessions and accomplishments. In order to feel even greater, he exercised generosity with whatever he felt was superfluous. In that way he put other people in a dependent and subordinate position, feeding his ego.

*Chesed* doesn't investigate to see who is the recipient; it just gives and gives. It would be compared to the parent who gives the child anything he or she wants. The child becomes a total spoiled brat; the cause, the parent. I mention this to clarify the position of *chesed.*

There was a major difference between the kindness of Avrohom and Yishmoel. Avrohom gave to everyone based on the guidance and direction of intellect. As we mentioned at great length earlier, this is called *middos al pi sechel,* which is the proper holy and godly way of being benevolent. On the other hand, Yishmoel was also very kind and benevolent. However, he didn't discriminate at all; he just expressed *middos* without the guidance of *sechel.* Therefore his *chesed* is called *chesed* of *klipah* negative and not godly.

When we say *chesed* is the abundance of lovingkindness, we must realize that this means in a proper way. For example, a person is homeless and asks for money. *Chesed* of Yishmoel would be to give him without investigating what he does with the money. *Chesed* of Avrohom would be to refrain from giving him money, rather to take him into a store and buy him food. Avrohom gives as well, the difference being, Avrohom uses his rational mind to discern between good and bad; therefore, instead of giving him money so that he can do whatever he so desires, Avrohom's approach is to very carefully help him by buying food for him, securing the fact that he will live another day. On the other hand, Yishmoel's approach is to give without asking questions. Just because it feels good to give indiscriminately doesn't mean it's right for the person receiving the kindness. In fact, many times what looks like a good act of kindness might be the totality of selfishness. Many times, instead of having a true interest in helping someone who is homeless, it is easier to take the short cut, just give to get rid of him. That's another aspect of Yishmoel's benevolence, selfishness with a facade of caring and concern.

The reason a person has a Torah obligation to use Avrohom's approach (and it is not considered arrogance even though it might look like invading someone else's privacy) is because it has been established that most people who are homeless use the money given to them to buy items that are dangerous to their very existence. So to just give from a soft spot in one's heart may produce good feeling but could result in assisting someone in hurting himself; and *he* doesn't feel good; nothing positive has been done for his character. So calling the *middah* of *chesed* one of the ten holy *sefiros* means the proper expression as exemplified by Avrohom. This form of *chesed* still retains its identity, which is to go out of its way to help someone whether or not help is deserved. However, *what* is given is very exact and focused.

What follows the first *sefirah* is *gevurah,* severe restraint. When a person is not deserving of help either because he himself is not fit to receive assistance or the circumstances are such that they do not warrant support, this precise and calculated approach is called *gevurah. Gevurah* is the antithesis of *chesed.* It completely shuts down any form of communication with anyone not worthy of help.

Another way of defining *gevurah* is judgment. For example, when the Torah mentions God creating the world, God's name used is Elokim, meaning judgment. The Torah uses the same term for a human judge, whose job it is to sit at a trial and render a verdict. What this means, as far as human experience is concerned, is the fact that the human tendency is to constantly stand in judgment of people, usually to find something wrong, tempting the "judge" to deny them the right of existing. This too is a very severe expression of *gevurah.*

Yet there is a third form of severe *gevurah* that is actually positive. This is the idea of *gevurah* coming from the concept of *gevuras geshomim,* the strength of the rain. Sometimes it just doesn't rain, it pours. Each raindrop is equivalent to an entire bucket of water. Chasidus explains that usually God gives an ordinary blessing, but there are times when the blessing from God is so powerful that it is comparable to *gevuras geshomim.* It is similar to what is written in the Prophets: "I'll give you so much blessing that your lips will say, enough, enough." This is another form of *gevurah.*

How is the third idea of *gevurah* different from *chesed?* It seems as if *gevurah* as well is an abundant amount of energy being given either to the world or from one person to another. The distinction between them is that the quality of *gevurah* is vigorous and deep, and *chesed* is bland and shallow. When a child is rejected and denied the right to participate in a particular activity due to his or her behavior, this will give a more permanent lesson to the child. In this form of *gevurah,* the parent is giving the child something that externally appears to be restraint, but what is really happening internally is that the parent is giving the child real and eternal strength. The discipline gained by the child is a lifelong possession. This would be analogous to the concept of *gevuras geshomim,* very powerful rain, in that the lesson here for the child is more powerful then the ordinary lesson learned by the child from his *chesed* experiences. On the other hand, acting with *chesed* appears at first glance to be the epitome of kindness, yet its impact on a child will not be as powerful. Since it was given from the parent to the child in the form of love, it tends to be more shallow and bland. In other words, *chesed* is the abundance of quantity and *gevurah* is the abundance of quality.

However, even after all is said and done, both *chesed* and *gevurah* are at odds with each other. The primary reason is that they are extremes. When two people in a relationship are extremists in their positions and ideologies, the relationship will most surely crumble and disintegrate. Therefore the third *sefirah,* known as *tiferes,* compassion and mercifulness, is a proper mediator and intermediary to bring out the best in both.

*Tiferes* literally means beauty. Take, for example, colors. When a color stands by itself it cannot be beautiful, regardless of its particular composition. However, an image composed of various colors, each in its proper place, can possess great beauty. The same is true in respect to the *middos.* Each *middah* on its own is not truly "beautiful," meaning it desires mending. The mending process is the combination of each other. How is this possible? It's through the *middah* of *tiferes,* which blends *chesed* and *gevurah.*

Take the example of a person not worthy of receiving kindness because he is truly not nice. Here are the three different responses: *Chesed* says, "I'll give you as much as you want; I won't discriminate." *Gevurah* says, "I'll give you nothing; you haven't earned it." *Tiferes* says, "I'll have compassion on you, and even though you don't deserve it, I'll give it to you anyway because I have mercy on you." What *tiferes* is doing is providing a platform for both *chesed* and *gevurah.* On one hand, the person is receiving, which would be a similar expression to *chesed.* On the other hand, the amount the person is receiving is minimal, because in truth he shouldn't be getting anything. It's just that the giver has mercy on the receiver and helps him. This is an expression of *gevurah,* to restrain and not give. The added *middah* of *tiferes* causes the person to go beyond the letter of the law and still help. However, as said before, it is a very limited amount that is being given. This makes the *middah* of *tiferes* really "beautiful." *Tiferes* is able to overcome the negativity of *gevurah* and at the same time is able to appease *gevurah* by giving less than what the person desires. Also, *tiferes* accommodates *chesed* by the fact that it gives and helps the person, and it doesn't allow *gevurah* to prevent it from helping at all. Therefore *tiferes* is a fine mediator and intermediary.

How does *tiferes* possess this talent? Chasidus answers this by teaching us that *tiferes* actually has a deeper connection with God than *chesed* and *gevurah.* This means *tiferes* expresses more of God's infinity and greatness than *chesed* and *gevurah.* An example to clarify the point: There are two officials working for the president of the United States. One is in charge of education and the other of transportation. Each one desires and lobbies that more money should be spent by the government on his particular task. They constantly are arguing with each other, always soliciting the president for more funds for their cause. Finally one day they are summoned by the president. They enter his room and for the first time they realize they both are equal representatives of the same president. They recognize that it is the president who has an interest in both education and transportation. In fact, his interest is equal, and he is loyal to both. They walk out shaking hands and agree to begin working together.

What happened here? How all of a sudden do they come to this recognition? The answer is that for the first time in their lives they stopped looking at each other as rivals and began viewing their roles as complementing each other, culminating in the best for the president. Who caused them to feel this way? It is the president. However, it is only when they come before the president and actually stand there that his overpowering presence causes them to be humble and submit to him by making up with each other. They realize this is the president's desire.

The same is true in the soul. *Chesed* and *gevurah* each have their own agenda. They contradict each other; they can't get along. *Tiferes,* since its source is associated with the infinity of God's essence, finds a way to make peace. That method is by letting them know that they both are working for the same God! They don't have to compete with each other. It is possible to live together. All it takes is the realization that *tiferes* is here, which is tantamount to God being here, God being the one who wants both *chesed* and *gevurah.*

This now sheds light on the greatness of *tiferes. Tiferes* isn't a combination of *chesed* and *gevurah.* Rather, *tiferes* is a separate *middah* that connects to a deeper aspect of God, more so than *chesed* and *gevurah.* It's only because *tiferes* is connected with the essence of God that it is able to combine opposites and find a way to allow both *chesed* and *gevurah* to coexist. This concept is called in Chasidus *tiferes ola ad ein sof, tiferes* ascends to the infinite. In practical terms, when a person can only be kind and not exercise restraint, this is a limitation. When a person is only strict and nongiving, this too is a limitation of his character. However, if a person is able to do both, this is a sign of a strong character. It shows that he is in total control. These three *middos* are known by their acronym, *Chagas,* meaning *chesed, gevurah,* and *tiferes.*

# 14

# *Netzach, Hod, Yesod,* and *Malchus:* Endurance, Adoration, Bonding, and Royalty

**Terms**

| | |
|---|---|
| *N'hym* | *Netzach, Hod, Yesod,* and *Malchus* |
| *Hodaah* | Acknowledgment |
| *Hishkashrus* | Bonding |
| *Mesiras Nefesh* | Total dedication of oneself to God |

*Na'utz tchiloson besofon vesofon betchiloson*
The beginning is wedged in the end and the end is
wedged in the beginning

| | |
|---|---|
| *Ko'ach mah* | The potential of "what" |

In Chasidus these four *sefiros* are known by their acronym, *N'hym.* These are the *sefiros* that take into consideration the outside world so that the more inward *sefiros* can fully express themselves. The person, the giver, is considered on the inside. For example, there is a teacher and a student. The teacher has to first realize that he is a teacher to a particular individual, which means he has to recognize that there is another world outside of himself, namely, the student. Once he comes to this realization, he has to think of means to contract his knowledge in a way that is compatible to him without overwhelming the student. In addition, the teacher has to feel good about his student so that his desire to share his information will be with joy and love. All of these steps are within the mind of the teacher before he says even one word to the student. At the actual time when the teacher is ready to communicate, he has to deliberate as to the exact words and phrases he will use so that the student understands exactly what the teacher means. Once this happens, the teacher begins bonding with the student and feeling a sense of unity. Finally the teacher forsakes his feelings and position of superiority and makes his student the primary focus realizing that the student is totally committed and devoted to him, through submitting himself to his teacher. This causes the teacher great satisfaction and pleasure, culminating with the teacher coming to the conclusion that "it's my student who has taught me more then anyone else."

The same details can be seen in a person's character. One is the "inside" state. This is total self-focus. The person expressing Chabad and *Chagas* is still focusing on self, developing intellectual components and refining emotional attributes, with self at the center of this important process. However, when the person reaches the state of the four character traits known as *n'hym,* he moves from focusing on self to the point where he begins thinking about others. He begins deliberating and asking himself, "How will people perceive me? Is what I am saying and doing befitting a character that is intellectually and emotionally sound?" This type of self-assessment is considered a reflection that takes into consideration the outside world, including the personal self that has a part that is "outside" in comparison to its "inside," which is its intellect and emotions.

In particular, the *middah* of *netzach* has several expressions. One is to be victorious over any obstacles that hinder doing what intellect and emotions say are correct. This includes the opposition of *gevurah. Gevurah* feels one doesn't deserve. *Netzach* says, "I'm going to motivate my power of victory and prevail," the result being the person wins the "war." Also, *netzach* means endurance, that is, the everlasting impact that the quality of *netzach* will have on character. All the other *middos* can fade away, but *netzach* is enduring.

The previous Lubavitcher Rebbe, Rebbe Yosef Yitzchok Schneerson, told the following parable to clarify the point: A king has many treasures that he inherited from his ancestors. They never have been opened. The reason is, the king knows that someday there will be a situation in which he will have to open those treasures in order to save his life and kingship. That day comes along; he finds himself in the middle of a war threatening his existence. At that time he opens the treasures and instructs his soldiers to take whatever they need to save him and his kingdom. This, the Rebbe says, is the true idea of *netzach,* to activate that part of a person that will do anything and everything to achieve his true purpose. One feels one is in a "war" with one's character. There are obstacles from the inside and from the outside. Therefore, using the last resort, which is the quality of *netzach,* will assure victory. This will also cause the victory to be enduring, since it comes from a place within that is very deep. It is so deep and concealed that it takes a war to reveal it. Therefore, once it is revealed and is operating, it uses its own qualities; these qualities go beyond the daily experience. Actions taken yesterday, or perceiving that one's character lacks refinement, don't prevent one from doing what one has to.

The next *middah* is *hod,* adoration and devotion. As mentioned earlier, both *netzach* and *hod* are the deliberating aspects within the person. *Netzach* deliberates by activating the sensation of victory ("I must prevail"), and *hod* deliberates based on adoration and devotion. In the teacher–student example, when the teacher adores his student, this causes the teacher to properly assess the student and not to overwhelm him and cause damage. This can only be realized by the teacher if he truly cares for the student. This adoration is one of the aspects of *hod.* The other aspect is devotion. When the teacher realizes the compliance and obedience that the student actually has, or that the student has the potential to devote himself to the teacher, this causes the teacher to communicate, very carefully, the right amount of information.

These two feelings that the teacher has toward the student can also be found in the student's feelings toward the teacher. First, the student develops an adoration and love for the teacher. Sometimes this feeling is motivated by the teacher, and sometimes it is motivated by the student's natural feelings toward the teacher. The second aspect of *hod,* as reflected by the student toward the teacher, is the devotion and obedience the student has. These two aspects of *hod* shed light on a Jew's relationship with God. First, he develops his character to have a feeling of love and adoration toward God. This attraction is based on the recognition that

God is King therefore beloved. Next follows a feeling of devotion through observing His commands and directives. Chasidus explains that *hod* comes from the word *hodaah,* meaning acknowledgment. When a person acknowledges God as the master of his personal universe and that God desires this devotion, this in turn activates a feeling of love, adoration, and devotion within the person's heart, resulting in a total devotion to God. This is the idea of *hodaah.*

This deliberation that *netzach* and *hod* provide aren't enough to guarantee an everlasting impact on character. It is only because of the *middah* called *yesod,* bonding, that a person's devotion to God or to another person is guaranteed. In Chasidus there is a unique emphasis on this idea. The test used to see if a *chasid* is truly dedicated to his or her rebbe is to analyze his *hiskashrus,* his bond to the rebbe. This notion of *hiskashrus* is the ultimate bond between *chasid* and rebbe. It transcends all barriers and limitations. Whether it be fire or water, the *chasid* is prepared to do everything and anything for his rebbe (needless to say, only those things that are permitted by Torah). *Hiskashrus* goes beyond the letter of the law.

For example, in the 1920s and 1930s the KGB would assign special surveillance agents to Jews who had prayer services and Torah classes in their homes. The previous Lubavitcher Rebbe demanded that his *chasidim* not be scared and continue going about their business of spreading Torah throughout Russia. Many of his contemporaries disagreed. They felt that the Torah did not require obedience that would put people's lives in danger. The Rebbe was very aware of this; however, he felt that true *hiskashrus* between a *chasid* and a rebbe means to go the extra mile to fulfill the rebbe's desires. Therefore just as he, the Rebbe, put his life on the line, he should demand the same of his *chasidim.* The *chasid* was glad that he had an opportunity to do what the Rebbe wanted. He felt that when he was chosen by the Rebbe to be in this position, his *hiskashrus* was being strengthened.

This is the unique quality of *yesod.* It reveals the person's deep connection to God. In human relationships, similar devotion may be found. But first, go back to the example of the teacher and his student. If the teacher wants his relationship to be eternal, it is not adequate that the deliberation used in communicating information be in a manner that just doesn't overwhelm the student; rather, the teacher must bond himself to the student. This bonding has many different forms, but the primary aspect is the mind-set of the teacher that says, "I'm yours and you're mine." When the student feels this radiance coming from the teacher, the student reciprocates a bond that will last forever.

In human relationships it is *hiskashrus,* bonding, that is the element within the character that causes the relationships to last. When two people have many things in common, but there is no bonding, this relationship will not last. Bonding in this scenario means to realize that the relationship's foundation is more than "we complement each other." The essence of bonding is to have a strong focus on each other, realizing that without each other neither is complete. In other words, they are two halves uniting. This is the power of bonding.

In regard to personal character traits, *yesod* is the element that bonds people to God and to the true essence within. In regard to God, *yesod* would be the concept of *mesiras nefesh,* total dedication of oneself to God. An example, mentioned earlier, is of the

Rebbe's directives to his *chasidim* to give their lives, if that's what it takes, on behalf of *Yiddishkeit,* Judaism. The concept of *yesod* within would be that feeling that there is no way that I can waive my responsibility to do what I know is correct. It is my bond to truth that makes me realize that without being truthful, I'm selling myself. This sensation comes directly from the attribute of *yesod.* I realize that without the truth, I'm only a half and my other half is missing. The bond to truth solidifies and secures a whole being, making it possible to assert character in a healthy way.

The last of the ten *sefiros* is *malchus,* royalty. Being the last *sefirah,* the teachings of Kabbalah explain that *malchus* is directly bound with the first *sefirah, chochmah.* In the terminology of the Kabbalah, *na'utz tchiloson besofon, vesofen betchiloson,* the beginning is wedged in the end, and the end is wedged in the beginning, that is, there is a special association between *malchus* and *chochmah. Chochmah,* as explained, is the element of conception, which does not yet have any definable form. Therefore *chochmah* is the "abode" with which God is able to identify. God, the epitome of *bittul,* humility, dwells only in "places" that express this notion of *bittul. Chochmah,* since it is not yet formed and comprehended, therefore, is the vessel for God. *Chochmah* is *bittul,* as the Hebrew word itself indicates; *chochmah* is a combination of two words, *ko'ach mah,* the "potential of what," since it is unknown what form *chochmah* is. *Malchus* has a similar quality. *Malchus,* the Kabbalah says, has "nothing of its own," *les lo migarma klum.* It has no flavor of its own. All it does is receive from the other nine *sefiros* above it and convey it to the next stage. *Malchus* is similar to a funnel in that it transfers things from one side to the other. This is again the idea of *bittul,* being a funnel and vessel for God without mixing in human understanding and ego. This is why the Kabbalah says that *chochmah* and *malchus* are wedged within each other.

How does the aspect of *malchus,* which is *bittul,* relate to royalty? It would seem that royalty is the antithesis to bittul. Chasidus explains this by analyzing royalty.

Look at a king. A king becomes a king by having subjects over whom he rules. A king isn't a king over ants and bugs; they don't serve his purpose. A king wants recognition and dominion. Ants don't have these qualities. Humans do. Therefore humans satisfy the king's desire. Thinking of a king this way leads to the conclusion that a king on his own without human subjects is worthless. That is correct. Since kingship and royalty are dependent on humans, this aspect of *malchus* is expressive of true *bittul.* Imagine a king soliciting his subjects to want him. This would cause everyone to seek another king. Why? Because royalty and kingship is a voluntary pursuit that people want. On the contrary, a king who has this element of *bittul* will have more followers. So that all of this makes it very clear, that the true strength of *malchus* is a feeling of *bittul.*

The following story illustrates the point: There was a chasidic rebbe who had many followers. A *misnadig* told him it was his ego and pride that pursued having so many *chasidim.* The *misnagid* said, "If you were truly humble, you would make a public announcement Friday night in *shul* when all your *chasidim* are present, telling everyone that you aren't a great rebbe and that they should go home; they have no reason to be in *shul* with a simpleton!" The rebbe said he would do exactly that. The next Friday night he made the announcement. The following week he had twice as many *chasidim!* This is the epitome of royalty-*bittul.*

This notion of *bittul* is an integral part of character. When a teacher communicates information in a condensed form after deliberation on which way he should actually convey it, and has focused in on the student, causing a bond between student and teacher, all of this is the teacher's perspective. To truly reach the student, the teacher has to put himself into the student's position, which is that of recipient. The teacher cannot "feel" the student's needs unless he strips himself from his way of thinking and starts thinking more in the terms of the student. This courageous act and mind-set that the teacher undergoes manifests a sense of *bittul.* The teacher puts himself aside, which includes his understanding, his pride, and his authority. This is an act of *bittul.* The student feels this commitment and self-sacrifice and reciprocates by totally becoming one with his teacher. In other words, the bonding that *yesod* creates is very much real, but it is from the teacher's perspective. *He* is bonding to the student and *he* is causing the student to bond with him.

The expression of *malchus* is very different. The *student* is causing the teacher to connect and dedicate himself to the student. It is coming from the student's vantage point. The remarkable thing is that this stimulus is part of the teacher's real feelings. This is the ultimate of *bittul,* a sensation of commitment to others, generated by others, yet felt within a person in a manner that allows the outside stimulus to drive him and guide him. These two approaches would be other examples of *milmaila limato,* from above to below, and *milmato limailo,* from below to above, mentioned earlier. *Yesod* in comparison to *malchus* would be *milmailo limato,* generated by the teacher's focus and bond to the student. *Malchus* in comparison to *yesod* would be *milmato limailo,* generated by the student being there as the primary target.

Now looking at *malchus* within the human character, it is the element of *bittul* that best allows a person to feel royal. Royalty isn't any one specific virtue; rather it's a feeling of regality that creates within all of one's character a royal feeling. This could compare to the idea of *taanug,* discussed earlier. One can't describe, to another, one's particular delights in a manner that the other person could actually say, "I know why and how this person feels during his fulfillment of his delights." The only thing the other can say is, "I realize that this person has been impacted by his delights. I can see that his mind, heart, and other character traits are totally uplifted in a way that never before has he been this way." The reason for this observation is that *taanug* impacts all parts of one's being without having one specific abode.

The same is true in regard to *malchus* as the personal tenth attribute. *Malchus* impacts all other nine character traits. The way it does it, is through royalty, which is by having this true feeling of *bittul. Bittul,* as far as the character is concerned, means to realize that God is everything and that the person is God's subject to fulfill His desire. When a person accomplishes this transformation, he feels royal in a very humble way. This feeling permeates all parts of the being; subsequently people see in the person a new person.

Put in other terms, *malchus* is the aspect of character that is a vessel for humility in that it recognizes that tooting one's own horn, even though that horn might be great and wonderful, is only limiting experience to refining the nine character traits. All these character traits are a development of the self. *Malchus* is a development of the non-ego drive within the character. This is the reason that God chose *malchus* as the final *sefirah:* it culminates God's true royalty. When God expresses Himself through all subjects including the human species, this is His greatest pleasure. *Malchus* is the element within the character that accomplishes this.

What all of the above points to is a strong need for a refinement of the ten *kochos hanefesh.*

# VI

# IMPLEMENTING THE SOUL'S BEAUTY

# 15

## *Machshovah, Dibbur,* and *Maisseh:* Thought, Speech, and Action

**Terms**

*Livushei hanefesh*     The "garments" of the soul
*Mihus ha'adom*     A person's essence
*Benoni*     The "average" person
*oilomos*     Worlds
*Atzilus, Briyah, Yetzirah,* and *Assiyah*
Closeness, Creation, Formation, and Action

The previous chapters explained at great length the *kochos hanefesh.* These attributes are also known as the *mahus ha'adom,* the person's true essence. Chasidus asserts that the *mahus ha'adom* doesn't change easily. Basically, a person is who he is. He was created with a certain way of thinking and feeling. However, what the person is able to change are thoughts, speech, and actions. Changing one's very essence and core can only happen if God grants a "gift." To clarify this requires understanding what are the outlets that the

*neshomah* has. In other words, *sechel* and *middos*
are part and parcel of one's very being; they have a
means by which they express themselves. This Chasidus calls the *livushei hanefesh,* the "garments" of the
soul. They consist of three: *machshovah* (thought),
*dibbur* (speech), *maisseh* (action). These three garments are analogous to clothing in that, just as clothing
can beautify a person, the nicer a person is dressed the
nicer he'll appear. The same is true in regard to the
spiritual garments for the soul. The more a person
refines thought, speech, and action, the nicer the person's character appears to be.

The reason the word *appears* is used is that just as
clothing doesn't change who one truly is, it doesn't
create a smarter or kinder person, so too the garments
of the soul don't change a person's essence. Rather,
they take what traits one possesses and bring them to
the forefront in a nice way. Through refining thoughts,
speech, and action, a person actually looks and appears
to be nicer, kinder, and more pleasant. This is the
reason the Alter Rebbe in the Tanya teaches that a
*benoni*—an average person—doesn't have the ability,
on a conscious level, to change his *middos* from bad to
good. All the *benoni* can accomplish is to subdue his
evil thoughts, to control his improper unrefined con-
versation, and to act in accordance with God's
directives.

How do these three *livushim* operate? Chasidus
explains this by introducing the following ideas. In
kabbalistic teachings there is a concept called *oilomos,*
meaning worlds. This refers to the creation of supernal
spiritual realms that express a certain degree of godly
unity. There are four worlds: (1) the world of *atzilus,*
total closeness with God; (2) the world of *briyah,*

creation; (3) the world of *yetzirah,* formation; and (4) the world of *assiyah,* action. In the realm of *atzilus,* the expression of godliness is felt in a manifested way. The word *atzilus* means close and adjoining. This expression of godliness is close and near to the subjects that exist in that state of consciousness. In the realm of *briyah,* God has removed Himself one step from being totally near His subjects. In fact, God has created something that appears to be "outside" Himself: a world that feels and thinks of itself outside and separate from God. This is the concept of creation ex nihilo, *yesh mei'ayin,* that we discussed earlier. The third manifestation of God is the plane of *yetzirah.* This is also called the world of formation. This means that not only has God given the potential for an entity outside of His total unity to exist, but even more so, this entity starts taking form and solidifying its status of concealing God. Finally, the fourth level of godliness is the world of *asiyah,* the realm of action. This means that not only is there a potential for a real physical world, and not only does it begin forming its own dynamics, but in this realm God is completely hidden. All that is felt is action. Action, without a realization that something had to make it possible for the act to happen, is a total denial that God made it happen. Chasidus explains that the fourth world of *asiyah* is still very much a spiritual concept. What follows from that is the creation of an actual physical universe in which God is concealed from the human eye.

All of these "worlds" are not only to be understood as metaphysical thoughts, which are removed from our real world. Rather they are very real ideas, right here on earth. Every individual can express and possess one or more of these four levels. All it takes is a conscious effort to recognize what is going on in life. For instance, when a person desires to be godly all the time by obeying God's commandments and not succumbing to corporeal temptations, this is an expression of *atzilus,* because the person is close and near God, and therefore he feels the unity every moment. On the other hand, when a person feels like doing God's will sometimes, but other times he feels like goofing off, this is an expression of the other three worlds, depending on how removed he is from God's presence. If the majority of the time he feels this way, he would be expressing the world of *yetzirah.* If this feeling is only a minority of the time, this would be a manifestation of the world of *briyah.* What all this points to is that these lofty esoteric ideas begin with our personal status, today, tomorrow, and so on.

Chasidus explain that the world of *briyah* is compared to *machshovah.* Just as thought is constant and totally private, so too does the notion of *briyah* represent a constant and private notion of creation. This means that the physical universe from *briyah's* perspective is still very much bound and connected to God in a way that doesn't allow for any separateness. This is why *machshovah* is called a *livush hamiyuched,* a designated constant garment; it is constantly working even during sleep. Thought doesn't stop until the last moment of life. In this sense thoughts are very private and are subordinate to *kochos hanefesh. Briyah* is the same way. It is the beginning of creation in that it has been removed from *atzilus,* but it is not yet identifiable because the godly energy of *atzilus* overshadows it. On the other hand, speech and action are compared to the worlds of *Yetzirah* and *assiyah. Yetzirah* is the formation and development of a world by exemplifying the radiance of God as a lead-in to reality. *Dibbur* also manifests this idea within the human framework. When a person talks, he is allowing someone outside of himself to become involved in his life.

The mere fact that the purpose of speech is that people can understand each other reveals two things: (1) speech isn't private in nature, and (2) speech is not continuous; sometimes people talk and sometimes they're quiet. In the same vein, *yetzirah* is such that it is yet another removal from the oneness of God. Therefore *yetzirah* isn't as close to God as is *briyah,* just as thought is further from a person's essence than is speech. Thought is constant and private, and speech is irregular and public. This is why speech is called a *livush hanifrad,* a garment that has been separated from the person. This garment isn't here just for the person, it is here for the outside as well.

Since *dibbur* is a *livush hanifrad, maisseh* is all the more a *livush hanifrad.* Action is entirely removed from the person's intellectual and emotional experience. Action requires more effort and is more intermittent than speech. It is also more public. Therefore *maisseh* is compared to *oilom ha'assiyah,* the world of action. In *oilom ha'assiyah,* godliness is completely concealed, yet at the same time it is *oilom ha'assiyah* that actualizes the reality of creation that began in *oilom habriyah.*

Now that we have a better understanding of the three garments of the soul, we can discuss their beautification. As mentioned before, the *benoni,* average person, isn't able to convert intellect or feelings to be totally good and excellent. That's the job of a *tzaddik,* a righteous person who is free from sin. However, most ordinary people are tempted to commit sins and transgress God's will. They are therefore "tested" daily, and the most they accomplish is to not allow their urges and emotions to carry them away. By refraining from transgressing God's will, they become *benonim,* meaning they have maximized their human potential and restrained themselves. When people do this, they are beautifying their thoughts, speech, and action. They do this by thinking proper thoughts, speaking words of kindness that intellectually are appropriate, and acting in a very nice way. Therefore the *benoni* is what Chasidus says to strive for. A *tzaddik's* level is beyond our capability and scope of reality. However, to be a *benoni,* this every person can attain; one doesn't have to have a special soul.

This is the reason Chasidus emphasizes the importance of refining the "garments." In other forms of Jewish thought there is a great emphasis on essence. Chasidus uses a different approach. Chasidus says make the focus the divine garments; they will help a person grow further and closer to God. As far as essence is concerned, humans really don't know what's going on. And besides, it shouldn't concern the human mind, because a person has been born that way and it's God's issue.

This idea can be understood with a story mentioned in the Talmud. Rabbi Yochanon Ben Zakai, prior to his passing on, said, "I don't know in which path I'm going to." He was referring to his afterlife. Was he going to Paradise, or, God forbid, to *Gehinom*—Purgatory? The question asked by many commentators is, how could Rav Yochanon not know? He was a real *tzaddik;* he never sinned; he would be fooling himself and be out of line to even think that he might end up being punished. The Lubavitcher Rebbe, Rabbi Menachem Mendel Schneerson, of blessed memory, gives the following response. Rav Yochanon throughout his lifetime was so busy and occupied in fulfilling his mission as a Jew that he felt it would be a pure waste of time to think about his personal status. Not only that but it would be considered a sin to think about his situation, because thinking about himself would be tantamount to wasting precious time that he needed to serve God by accomplishing, not focusing on himself. However, when came the day of his passing, he had a Torah obligation to make an account of his entire lifetime. Therefore, this was the first time in his entire life that he actually stopped to think about himself! So of course he didn't know—he never thought about it!

This real episode isn't just a fable, rather, it has a very profound lesson for each and every person. When people spend time and energy focusing on themselves, thinking about their good qualities and their shortcomings, if this involves questions like, "Why do I have a certain type of mind?" or "Why didn't God create me with a nicer character?" These issues are a pure waste of time. This is an arrogant approach to becoming a better Jew and person. People should stop focusing on self and begin focusing on God. How? God wants Jews to refine and improve their way of thinking. Their words should be more godly and their actions need to be a resemblance of a Jew. This is the Jewish task and responsibility. A *benoni* has perfected the self in regard to the three *livushim.* Therefore, the *benoni* is the ultimate refined human being in God's creation.

This shows the importance of *maisseh,* action. There is a chasidic saying: "Think little, speak even less, and do more." It's important to think and speak, but it's most important to act. As the saying goes, *hamaiseh hu ha'ikar,* action is the main thing.

# 16

# *Iskafya* and *Isapcha:*
# Subjugation and
# Transformation

**Terms**

*Lishem shomaiyim*    For the sake of heaven (God)
*Sefer shel benonim*   The book for the average person
*Sefer shel tzaddikim*  The book for the righteous

Not only does Chasidus place great emphasis on refining the *neshomah* so that its beauty is apparent, but in addition, Chasidus supplies the tools to successfully implement this beauty. Specifically, two terms are used. One is *iskafya,* meaning to subdue and to subjugate, and the second term is *isapcha,* to transform and convert. These ideas refer to daily involvement with mundane affairs. To take a simple example, a person is served a meal. She knows that the Torah wants of her to eat the food *lishem shomaiyim,* for the sake of heaven, meaning the food should be eaten for the purpose of strengthening her connection to God, not just to fill her appetite or to indulge. However, the delicious food

133

tempts her to just indulge. Here she has two methods of elevating herself and the food. The first way is by not eating it at all; since she feels incapable of eating the food in a manner that will allow her to be in control, she must go away from the situation, that is, the food, and restrain herself from indulging. In other words, she isn't strong enough to be present in a situation in which she has the temptation before her eyes.

The second approach is to have the emotional strength to actually eat the food in a way that she elevates herself and the food. This she accomplishes by realizing that the food, good and delicious as it may taste to the palate, has as its only true purpose to be eaten in a manner that makes her healthier and stronger so that she is able to serve God. This task necessitates real strength. Here she is challenged and confronted by a situation that demands she face the issue, not run away, and actually get involved, yet retain her integrity and have it impact the food.

Put more simply: A person is served a food dish that's missing salt. It tastes pretty lousy. How does she react? It depends on her perspective. Someone not strong enough emotionally to deal with the situation will complain and make a big scene. In short, she won't eat the unsalted food. On the other hand, a person who has refined herself will eat it and realize that the truth of the matter is that whether or not it has salt is insignificant, because the primary thing is to eat the food to become healthier and stronger in order to serve God. So what is the real difference whether or not it is salted? It's just a desire of the palate to want it to taste just right. To go ahead and eat means dealing with the lousy situation and succeeding. It's as though the food has salt. The only way to truly feel this way is by elevating oneself and realizing that there is more to life than what tastes and looks good.

These two down-to-earth approaches are called *iskafya* and *isapcha*. *Iskafya* means to subdue and to subjugate, to withhold oneself from a given difficult situation, because one isn't able to deal with it since it is in control. *Isapcha* means to transform and convert the difficulty by getting involved with the situation, yet the person is in full control. In Kabbalah the concept of *isapcha* is mentioned in regard to transforming darkness to light and bitterness to sweetness. Sometimes darkness and light exist as two entities, each in their own realms. However, to take the very darkness itself and have it become light is a great feat. To take a negative and transform it so that it becomes positive reveals that the only reason for the negative was to challenge, to see if indeed a person has the strength to face the temptation and convert it. The same is true in regard to taking something that is bitter and changing it so that it becomes sweet. Just think of taking a food item that is bitter in its taste, and somehow by adding the right flavors and ingredients, it becomes sweet. This is what the Kabbalah means when it says, "from bitterness to sweetness."

Chasidus explains the idea of *iskafya* by reminding Jews of the way in which the Hebrews left Egypt. The Midrash teaches that the Jewish ancestors were immersed in idol worship. Along came Moses, based on God's instructions, and informed them that they were going to be taken out of exile by God on the fifteenth of *Nisan*. The Jewish people couldn't believe it. They looked at themselves and knew that they were not worthy of this great favor—they were actively involved in idolatry! Yet it happened. The Hebrews became a free people, leading to the creation of the Jewish people. The Torah in describing the episode uses the words *ki borach ha'am,* meaning the nation fled and ran away from the Egyptians. Chasidus asks why it was necessary to run away. After all, wasn't God taking them out? Wasn't God's protection strong enough to guard them from any danger? The explanation given is that they weren't strong enough. Their minds and hearts were involved with nonsense. To have attempted to deal with the Egyptian culture, to reject intellectually the pagan practices, would have failed, because the Jews from their perspective couldn't deal with this difficult situation; they were in a sense "Egyptianized." Therefore the only solution was to vacate and flee, which they did. God, knowing their capabilities, gave Moses the instruction to command them to just go and not think about possessions, houses, and saying good-bye to neighbors.

Chasidus teaches that the service of the *benoni* consists of *iskafya.* This means that the *avodah,* service, of *isapcha* isn't expected of the *benoni.* This idea is very relevant to any Jew, because each and every one can be a *benoni.* Therefore, the *avodah* of *iskafya* is expected of every Jew. As mentioned in earlier chapters, the *benoni* is the state of being that perfects thought, speech, and action. The Alter Rebbe in Tanya teaches that in general every Jew is the type of person who is obligated to pursue becoming a *benoni.* God doesn't ask of anyone to convert intellect or emotions from being who and what they are. However, to properly manifest them in a way that improves thoughts, speech, and action is the responsibility. This is one of the reasons the book of *Tanya* is called *Sefer shel Benonim,* the book for the average person. The Alter

Rebbe had written a book called *Sefer shel Tzaddikim,* the book for the righteous; however, it was burned in an unexpected fire. The accepted tradition of why this happened is that people weren't ready to become *tzaddikim.* Therefore, in a sense its purpose and message weren't relevant. On the other hand, the *Tanya* is for everyone; therefore, it remained until today, being studied by thousands of people.

A *benoni* can perfect thoughts, speech, and action. As the Talmud says, God doesn't expect of a person to do something that is beyond his or her capability. If God asks that it be done, this is the best proof that it can be done. The *avodah* of *iskafya,* to hold back from indulging, this is expected of everyone. No person can say, "I can't do it; it's too difficult for me." The fact that a person has a temptation enter his mind, this he cannot help. However, what he can do is to immediately not allow the negative thought of indulging to dwell within the mind and subsequently the heart.

The *avodah* of a *tzaddik* is *isapcha,* to transform the negative. In fact, a *tzaddik* has already transformed his feelings of the heart that are nongodly and has converted those intellectual ideas that are contrary to God's will and wisdom. As King David says in Psalms, "My heart is hollow within me" (Psalm 109:22), meaning, "I've eliminated my evil inclination; I don't have any desire to sin!" Therefore, a *tzaddik* is called *Eved Hashem,* a servant of God.

This concept of *iskafya,* which is expected of every person, is the intrinsic meaning of the word *avodah.* The word itself comes from the talmudic statement, *"Oiros avudim,"* meaning refined skins. This refers to the work of a tanner in which the tanner takes very rough and course pieces of hide and works on them, the result being a nice smooth finish that is fit for use by human beings. The same is true regarding our *avodas Hashem,* our service to God. It's not enough to serve God with objects and items that are naturally positive. That's very easy since it is natural for anyone. However, when one serves God with items and issues in his life that are difficult to elevate to God, and works on himself and goes beyond natural tendencies, this shows that he isn't taking the easy way out. Therefore he is called an *oved Elokim,* a servant of God. All of this emphasizes the point that the implementation of the *neshomah* is through the *avodah* of *iskafya* and *isapcha.*

# Epilogue

With the help of God, I hope I've been able to help you open up your minds and hearts to the deep and important teachings of Chasidus. In no way is this book complete, rather, as a primer on the basic concepts and language of Chasidus, it is intended to whet the appetite for more. As I mentioned in one of the previous chapters, many times a specific topic is mentioned in brief in one chapter but will be discussed at length in another chapter. It is you, my dear student, whom I ask for feedback. I'm subjective, you are objective; please inform me in regard to the clarity of the ideas presented.

With the help of God, I hope that this book is just the first volume of several. Chasidus is one with God, therefore its ideas, principles, and terms are limitless in regard to their understanding. I also didn't write about many kabbalistic terms mentioned in Chasidus. I chose to dwell on the more practical terms. I hope, with the help of God, to cover more of these abstract kabbalistic terms in my next volume.

May we all see the perfection of these ideas in a down-to-earth way through the coming of our righteous *Moshiach,* when we will all have health, happiness, and prosperity, culminating with God's knowledge filling the earth, Amen.

# Appendix
# Questions for Review

## CHAPTER 1

1. Explain the approach of *halbashah* in regard to intellect.
2. Explain the approach of *hafshotah* in regard to *halbashah*.
3. Is every *metzius mugdar?*
4. What would be the *hagdarah* (limitation) of *hafshotah?*
5. If you have knowledge of something, how is it possible to divest yourself of it?
6. If you don't have knowledge of something, how is it possible to be invested in it?
7. Would you consider your approach to life *halbashah* or *hafshotah?*
8. Is the *etzem hanefesh mugdar?*
9. Explain *b'ma shehu* and *b'ma sheino.*
10. Which is easier to attain, *halbashah* or *hafshotah?* Explain why and how.

141

## CHAPTER 2

1.  Explain the verse *"kirvat Elokim li tov."*
2.  Which is more subjective, *sechel* or *middos?* How?
3.  Which is more objective, *sechel* or *middos?* How?
4.  What is *sechel?*
5.  What are *middos?*
6.  What are *middos al pi sechel?*
7.  Was it easy for Abraham to force his guests to thank God? Explain.
8.  Is the behavior of *middos al pi sechel* cold or warm? Explain.
9.  Does an animal have intellect? What kind?
10. What is true love from a Torah perspective?


## CHAPTER 3

1.  What does the *becheyn* mean?
2.  Explain the *becheyn* in regard to *sechel* and *middos.*
3.  What is the *becheyn* in regard to *guf* and *neshomah?*
4.  What is the *becheyn* in regard to *nigleh* and *nister?*
5.  What is the *becheyn* in regard to Torah and *mitzvos?*
6.  How is Chasidus the *becheyn* of Torah study?
7.  Explain *choref umaksheh.*
8.  Explain *musoon umasik.*
9.  What are the three meditations when making an account of your status?
10. How does the knowledge of an ultimate truth impact you?

## CHAPTER 4

1. Give an example of *mimaleh kol almin*.
2. Give an example of *sovev kol almin*.
3. Which impacts you more, *mimaleh* or *sovev?* How?
4. Explain the comparison between the servant–master relationship and *sovev.*
5. How is *taanug* compared to *sovev?*
6. How is Torah compared to *mimaleh?*
7. How are *mitzvos* compared to *sovev?*
8. Explain the concept of *shefa.*
9. How do *or* and *keli* help us understand *mimaleh* and *sovev?*
10. How can you attain *sovev kol almin* in your life?

## CHAPTER 5

1. What is the difference between *ratzon* and *taanug?*
2. Which influences the other? How?
3. Explain *hamshochas hanefesh.*
4. How do we see the concept of *ratzon* in the example of servant and master?
5. How do we see the concept of *taanug* in the example of servant and master?
6. Why and how does *ratzon* respond?
7. Why and how does *taanug* respond?
8. Why are they considered *kochos makifim?*
9. What does *kabbalas ol* mean?
10. Do you feel you have *kabbalos ol?* How?

## CHAPTER 6

1. How is nature an expression of *mimaleh kol almin?*
2. How are *nissim* a manifestation of *sovev kol almin?*
3. How is *ein baal hanes makir b'niso* an expression of *atzmus?*
4. How is *taanug* analogous to *atzmus?*
5. How is *taanug* analogous to *ein baal hanes makir b'niso?*
6. How can *teva* be a *keli* to *atzmus?*
7. What does *teva* connote?
8. How can a thief pray to God to help him steal?
9. With which of these three aspects do you function? Explain.
10. What is the difference between *Anochi,* Hashem, and *Elokecha?*


## CHAPTER 7

1. What are the Who, What, and Why of *dirah bitachtonim?*
2. Why didn't the creation of spiritual worlds suffice for God's purposes?
3. State the two meanings of ". . . since they [the spiritual realms] are a descent . . ."
4. What is the reason the Midrash chose the word *nisaveh* instead of *ratzah?*
5. What is the meaning *af ah taive iz nit kein kashah?*
6. Does an *etzem* possess parts?
7. Could God have created the world from *giluim*'s perspective?
8. Describe the virtue of God's name, *Mah?*

9. What impact does this divine name have on the human being?
10. What is more important, a *dirah* or a *lichtiker dirah?*

## CHAPTER 8

1. State and explain the negative aspects of the *nefesh habahamis.*
2. State and explain the positive qualities of the *nefesh habahamis.*
3. What is a soul?
4. What is the primary modus operandi of the *nefesh habahamis?* Explain.
5. What is the ancillary operative mode of the *nefesh habahamis?* Explain.
6. How does the *koa'ch ha'misaveh* operate?
7. What productivity do animals have that supersedes a human's ability?
8. What Torah values can be derived from animals?
9. Why indeed did the Torah instruct us regarding certain *mitzvos,* when we can come to the same conclusion by observing animals?
10. How do you plan on harnessing your *nefesh habahamis?*

## CHAPTER 9

1. What is the *nefesh hasichlis?*
2. How is it different from the *nefesh habahamis?*
3. What does *yesh mei'ayin* mean?
4. Why is God called *ayin?*
5. Why is the world called *yesh?*
6. What do *milmato limailo* and *milmailo limato* mean?

7. What do *isarusa d'leilu* and *d'litato* mean?
8. What are the different approaches to *teshuvah?*
9. Why is *bichirah* dependent on the *nefesh hasichlis?*
10. Are we the *nefesh ha'elokis, habahamis,* or *hasichhlis?* Explain.

## CHAPTER 10

1. What is the *Nefesh ha'elokis?*
2. What does *chelek eloka mimaal mamash* mean? Explain.
3. What is the difference between an angel and a soul?
4. Are gentiles able to be as spiritual as Jews? Explain.
5. What is the role of a gentile?
6. What does *Elokus shenaaseh nivreh* mean?
7. How can a *neshomah* go beyond its own limitations?
8. What is *klipas nogah?* What is *sholosh klipos hatimeios?*
9. What does *ko'ach hamafli laasos* mean?
10. What are *ratzu* and *shuv?*

## CHAPTER 11

1. What are the components of the *nefesh ha'elokis?*
2. What are the components of the *nefesh habahamis?*
3. What are the components of the *nefesh hasichlis?*
4. Why should we begin the process of *tikkun* with the *nefesh hasichlis?* How?
5. How do we change the nature of the *nefesh ha'elokis?*
6. How do we change the nature of the *nefesh hasichlis?*

7. Explain the accomplishment of Chasidus.
8. Who is an *eved* of God?
9. Who is an *oved* of God?
10. What is the difference?

## CHAPTER 12

1. Why is it important to meditate?
2. What is the purpose of the ten *sefiros?*
3. What is *chochmah?*
4. What is *binah?*
5. What is *daas?*
6. Can you have *daas* without *binah?* Why or why not? How? Explain.
7. Explain the different qualities of *daas.*
8. What is the significance of the word *daas* used in the *amidah?*
9. When is someone called a *maven?*
10. What do you consider yourself, a *Chocham, maven,* or *daiton (daas)?*

## CHAPTER 13

1. What is *chesed?*
2. What is *gevurah?*
3. What is *tiferes?*
4. What is the difference between the *chesed* of Avrohom and the *chesed* of Yishmoel?
5. Explain the three different aspects of *gevurah.*
6. Give an example to explain the concept of *gevuras geshomim.*
7. How does *tiferes* bring together *chesed* and *gevurah?*

8. What is the essence of *tiferes?*
9. Why are these *middos* called *chitzonius hanefesh?*
10. Why are Chabad called *pnimius hanefesh?*

## CHAPTER 14

1. Explain how *netzach* and *hod* are deliberators.
2. What are the two concepts of *netzach?* Explain.
3. What are the two ideas of *hod?* Explain.
4. What are the different aspects of *yesod?*
5. Explain *N'hym* in the example of the teacher and student.
6. What are the two concepts of *malchus?*
7. How is *malchus* a vessel for God?
8. How can you be royal and have *bittul* at the same time?
9. Explain the progression of the *sefiros.*
10. Which character traits do you excel in? Which do you need improvement in? Explain.

## CHAPTER 15

1. What is the *mahus ha'adom?*
2. Why are they called the *mahus ha'adom?*
3. What is the specialty of *machshovah?*
4. What is the advantage that *dibbur* has that *machshovah* doesn't have?
5. What is a *benoni?*
6. Explain the four *oilomos.*
7. What are the three *oilomos* that are compared to the three *livushim?* How?
8. Why didn't Rabbi Yochanon know where he was going after his passing?

9. What's the big deal with *maisseh?*
10. How can you become a *benoni?*

## CHAPTER 16

1. What is *iskafya?*
2. What is *isapcha?*
3. What does the *avodah* of *lishem shomaiyim* mean?
4. Give an example for *iskafya.*
5. Give an example for *isapcha.*
6. What is an *eved Elokim?* What is an *oved Elokim?*
7. What is the difference?
8. What is the difference between the *sefer shel Benonim* and *Sefer shel Tzadikim?*
9. Compare the *avodos* of *Iskafya* and *Isapcha.* Who does each?
10. What is the concept of *Avodah?*

# Glossary

An asterisk indicates a cross-reference within this glossary.

All non-English entries are Hebrew unless otherwise indicated.

*alul* (lit., "effect"): in chasidic terminology, the recipient in a downward flux of energy

*Assiyah* (lit. "deed"): in kabbalistic terminology, the lowest of the four spiritual worlds, the realm of spiritual existence that relates directly to our material world.

*Atik:* a lofty spiritual rung, the inner dimension of the level of *Keser*

*Atzilus* (lit. "emanation"): in kabbalistic terminology, the highest of the four spiritual worlds, the realm of spiritual existence which, although encompassing

151

attributes that have a specific definition, is completely at one with the *Or Ein Sof*

*avodah* (lit., "service"): formerly, the sacrificial service in the Temple, and later, the service of prayer instituted in its stead. In chasidic usage, this term refers to a person's striving for personal refinement and his efforts to establish unity between his spiritual ideals and his actual day-to-day operational consciousness

*baal teshuvah* (lit. "master of return"): a person who turns to God in repentance, after willful or unknowing transgression of the Torah's commandments

*b'drech memeila* (lit. "effortlessly"): used as a contrast to *hislabshus,* this term refers to an effusion of light or energy that reveals the source as it is, without considering the limitations of the recipient

*Binah* (lit., "understanding"): second of the ten *sefiros,* and second of the three intellectual powers; the power that develops a concept into depth and breadth

*bittul* (lit. "self-nullification"): a term used in two different contexts: with regard to spiritual existence, the nullification caused by the influence of a higher level; with regard to an individual's divine service, the efforts to rise above one's personal concerns and dedicate one's energies toward a higher goal or level of awareness

*Beis HaMikdash:* the Temple in Jerusalem

*Beriah* (lit. "creation"): more specifically creation *ex nihilo;* in kabbalistic terminology, the second of the four spiritual worlds, the realm of spiritual existence that represents the first beginnings of a consciousness of self

*Chabad* (acronym for the Hebrew words meaning "wisdom, understanding, and knowledge"): the approach to *Chasidism that filters its spiritual and emotional power through the intellect; a synonym for *Chabad* is Lubavitch, the name of the town where this movement originally flourished

*chasid* (pl., *chasidim*): adherent of the chasidic movement (see *Chasidus*)

chasidism: see *Chasidus*

*Chasidus:* chasidism, i.e., the movement within Orthodox Judaism founded in White Russia by R. Yisrael, the Baal Shem Tov (1698–1760), and stressing emotional involvement in prayer; service of God through the material universe; wholehearted earnestness in divine service; the mystical in addition to the legalistic dimension of Judaism; the power of joy and of music; the love to be shown to *every* Jew, unconditionally; and the mutual physical and moral responsibility of the members of the informal chasidic brotherhood, each *chasid* having cultivated a spiritual attachment to their saintly and charismatic leader, the Rebbe; the philosophy and literature of this movement; see also *Chabad*

*Chochmah* (lit., "wisdom"): the first of the ten *sefiros,* or divine emanations; the first stage of the intellectual process; the seminal point of a conceptual idea

*Elohim:* one of the names of God. In particular, this name is associated with the divine attributes that hold back, limit, and conceal godly influence so that it can descend and ultimately be enclothed within the limited context of worldly existence

*Gan Eden* (lit. "the Garden of Eden"): also used to refer to the abode of the souls in the spiritual realms in their afterlife

*Gemara:* the second part of the *Talmud; the elucidation of the *Mishnah;* and the discussion of related concepts by the Sages

*halachah* (pl., *halachos*): (a) the body of Torah law; (b) a particular law

*Havayah*—The term *Havayah* is derived from a rearrangement of the letters of the name h-w-u-y which, because of its holiness, is not pronounced in the usual manner. The name of God is associated with the divine attributes that reveal infinite godly light

*hishtalshelus:* the chainlike sequence of spiritual realms that allows for a progressive descent and contraction of divine light

*hislabshus* (lit., "enclothing"): the vesting of divine life energy in an entity in a manner that the divine life energy adapts itself to the level and condition of the recipient

*ikvesa diMeshicha:* the age directly before *Mashiach*'s coming when His approaching footsteps can be heard

*ilah* (lit., "cause"): in chasidic terminology, the first phase in a downward progression of energy

*kav* (lit. "line"): the vector of divine light that emanated after the first *tzimtzum*

*Keser* (lit., "crown"): the sublime level of divine emanation that transcends the set of the ten *sefiros;* in man's spiritual personality it is the source of the corresponding "superconscious" faculties of pleasure and will

*ko'ach* (lit., "potential"): a source of energy or force as it exists in a potential state

*Likkutei Torah:* a collection of chasidic discourses by Rabbi Shneur Zalman of Liadi, the Alter Rebbe

*maamar* (pl., *maamarim;* lit., "word"): in *Chabad* circles means a formal chasidic discourse first delivered by a rebbe

*Malchus* (lit., "sovereignty"): the last of the seven divine attributes and of their corresponding mortal spiritual emotions

*maor:* the source from which light, *or,* emanates

*Mashiach* (lit., "the anointed one"): the Messiah

*mazal:* in the context of the *maamar,* "source of influence," the soul as it exists in the spiritual realms, which exerts influence over the soul as it is enclothed in the body

*memaleh kol almin* (lit. "filling all worlds"): God's immanent light, which enclothes itself in every particular created being

*menorah:* the candelabra in the *Beis HaMikdash*

*mesiras nefesh* (lit., "sacrifice of the soul"): the willingness to sacrifice oneself, either through martyrdom, or through a selfless life, for the sake of the Torah and its commandments

*Midrash:* classical collection of the Sages' homiletical teachings on the Bible

*mikveh:* a ritual bath in which a person immerses himself as part of the transition from purity to impurity, or from a lower state of holiness to a higher state.

*Mishnah:* the first compilation of the Oral Law authored by Rabbi Yehudah HaNasi (approx. 150 C.E.). It serves as the basis for the Talmud

*Mitzrayim* (lit., "the land of Egypt"): figuratively, a state of limitation

*mitzvah* (pl., *mitzvos;* lit., "command"): a religious obligation; one of the Torah's 613 Commandments

*modim* (lit., "we thankfully acknowledge"): one of the blessings of the *Amidah* during which Jews are required to bow

Moshe Rabbeinu (lit., "Moses our Teacher")

*Nasi:* (a) in biblical times, the head of any one of the Twelve Tribes; (b) in later generations, the civil and/or spiritual head of the Jewish community at large

*or* (lit. "light"): an allegory for the effusion of godly energy and influence; the relationship between the *oros* and the *keilim* ("vessels") parallels that which exists between the body and the soul

*Or Ein Sof:* God's infinite light. The intent of this name is not merely that this light reveals God who is the True Infinity but that the light itself is infinite in nature

*po'el:* the activity resulting when a *koach* is manifest

*Radak:* an acronym for Rav David Kimchi, one of the foremost biblical commentators

*Sefirah* (pl. *Sefiros*): the kabbalistic term for the attributes of godliness that serve as a medium between His infinite light and our limited framework of reference

*sovev kol almin* (lit. "encompassing all worlds"): God's transcendent light, which reveals His unbounded nature

*Talmud:* the basic compendium of Jewish law, thought, and biblical commentary, comprising *\*Mishnah* and *\*Gemara;* when unspecified refers to the *Talmud Bavli,* the edition developed in Babylonia and edited at end of the fifth century C.E.; the *Talmud Yerushalmi* is the edition compiled in *Eretz Yisrael* at end of the fourth century C.E.

*Tanya:* the classic text of *\*Chabad* chasidic thought authored by the Alter Rebbe

*teshuvah* (lit., "return [to God]"): repentance

*Torah Or:* a collection of chasidic discourses by Rabbi Shneur Zalman of Liadi, the Alter Rebbe

*tzaddik:* righteous man

*tzedakah:* charity

*tzimtzum:* the process of divine self-contraction and self-limitation that makes possible the concept of limited, worldly existence

*yesh* (lit., "it exists"): in chasidic terminology, an entity that is limited and self-conscious *yesh me'ayin* (lit., "something from nothing"): creation *ex nihilo*

*yeshus:* the state of being a \**yesh*

*Yetzirah* (lit., "formation"); in kabbalistic terminology, the third of the four spiritual worlds, the realm of spiritual existence in which the limited nature of the created beings takes on form and definition

*Zaer Anpin* (Arm., lit, "the small face"): the term used by the *Kabbalah* for the divine attributes that parallel emotions

*Zohar* (lit. "radiance"): the title of the classic mystical work embodying the teachings of the *Kabbalah*

# Suggested Readings

Kagan, Y. M. *Thought for the Week.* Vols. 1–12. New York: Kehot, 1950–1990.

Mindel, Nissan. *The Commandments.* New York: Kehot, 1961.

Mindel, Nissan. *My Prayer: A Commentary on the Daily Prayers.* New York: Kehot, 1972.

Mindel, Nissan. *Philosophy of Chabad.* New York: Kehot, 1973.

Mindel, Nissan. *Rabbi Shneur Zalman of Liadi.* New York: Kehot, 1969.

Schneersohn, Rabbi Joseph I. *Chassidic Discourses.* Translated by Sholom B. Wineberg. Vols. 1–2. New York: Kehot, 1986.

Schneersohn, Rabbi Joseph I. *Memoirs.* Translated by Nissan Mindel. Vols. 1–2. New York: Kehot, 1956, 1960.

Schneersohn, Rabbi Joseph I. *On Learning Chassidus.* Translated with supplements by Zalman I. Posner. New York: Kehot, 1961.

Schneersohn, Rabbi Joseph I. *On the Teachings of Chassidus.* Translated with supplements by Zalman I. Posner. New York: Kehot, 1959.

Schneersohn, Rabbi Joseph I. *Some Aspects of Chabad Chassidism.* Translated with biographical sketch by Nissan Mindel. New York: Kehot, 1961.

Schneerson, Rabbi Menachem M. *Likkutei Sichot.* שליט"א. Translated by Jacob I. Schochet. Vols. 1–2. New York: Kehot, 1980, 1983.

Schneerson, Rabbi Menachem M. *Torah Studies: Adaptation of Sichos Given by the Lubavitcher Rebbe.* New York: Kehot, 1986.

Schneersohn, Rabbi Sholom DovBer. *Kuntres Uma'ayon.* Translated by Zalman I. Posner. New York: Kehot, 1978.

Schochet, Jacob I. *The Great Maggid: The Life and Teachings of Rabbi Dov Ber of Mezritch.* New York: Kehot, 1978.

Schochet, Jacob I. *Mystical Concepts in Chassidism.* New York: Kehot, 5739.

Zalman, Rabbi Shneur. *Likutei Amarim (Tanya).* Bilingual Edition. New York: Kehot, 1973.

# Index

# ABOUT THE AUTHOR

Chaim Dalfin received his rabbinical ordination from the Central Yeshiva Tomchei Temimim Lubavitch in Brooklyn, New York. He received his Bachelor of Religious Studies degree from the Rabbinical College of America in Morristown, New Jersey. Rabbi Dalfin is currently director of the Jewish Enrichment Center, dedicated to rejuvenating the hearts and minds of the young and old. He is the author of *Your Better Self* (1994), a book on the chasidic approach to self-improvement. Rabbi Dalfin developed his writing and speaking style after years of apprenticeship, learning from one of the greatest chasidic teachers of our generation, Rabbi Yoel Kahan. He also was a student of Rabbi M. M. Schneerson, the Lubavitcher Rebbe, of blessed memory. Rabbi Dalfin lectures nationwide on the fundamentals of Chasidus and also leads *farbrengens* with song, stories, and words of inspiration. A practicing rabbinic counselor, Rabbi Dalfin lives in Los Angeles, California, with his wife and four children.